SEEKING *the* SECRET PLACE

SEEKING *the* SECRET PLACE

The Spiritual Formation of C. S. Lewis

LYLE W. DORSETT

BrazosPress
Grand Rapids, Michigan

Published by Brazos Press
a division of Baker Publishing Group
P.O. Box 6287, Grand Rapids, MI 49516-6287
www.brazospress.com

Printed in the United States of America

Library of Congress Cataloging-in-Publication Data
Dorsett, Lyle W.
    Seeking the secret place : the spiritual formation of C. S. Lewis / Lyle W. Dorsett.
        p.   cm.
    Includes bibliographical references.
    ISBN 1-58743-122-X (pbk.)
    1. Lewis, C. S. (Clive Staples), 1898–1963—Religion. I. Title.
BX5199.L53D67 2004
230'.092—dc22   2004013887

All unpublished primary sources, including letters and oral history interviews, are housed in the Marion E. Wade Center, Wheaton College, Wheaton, IL, unless otherwise noted.

All published sources are available in the Wade Center.

All unpublished letters written by C. S. Lewis and quoted in this book are from *Letters by C. S. Lewis*, copyright © C. S. Lewis Pte. Ltd. Reprinted by permission.

First for my wife, Mary Hayes Dorsett,
who is still my closest and most trusted friend
as well as the love of my life.

This book is also dedicated
to two of my cherished friends,
Carol Kraft and Marjorie Lamp Mead.

Without you three saints
I could never have written this book.

CONTENTS

ACKNOWLEDGMENTS

This relatively short book has a rather long history. Many people have provided assistance along the way, but three people have been indispensable to its long preparation process: Mary Dorsett, Carol Kraft, and Marjorie Mead. To explain, I must go back to the 1980s.

In 1981, while conducting research for a biography of Helen Joy Davidman, C. S. Lewis's wife, I began interviewing people who knew her. In the midst of this oral history research it became surprisingly evident that no one had embarked upon the larger effort of systematically and carefully recording the reminiscences of C. S. Lewis's surviving relatives, friends, and associates. As a historian, I found this to be a distressing revelation. Therefore, one evening after concluding research on Joy Davidman at Wheaton College's Marion E. Wade Center, I sat down to ask a few last-minute questions of Marjorie Mead, the able associate director of the world's most extensive collection of Lewisiana. I suggested to her that it would be beneficial for the Wade Center and for me to interview Joy's son and C. S. Lewis's stepson, Douglas Gresham, on videotape. Douglas's brother,

David, freely answered my questions by mail, but he declined a personal interview. Douglas, on the other hand, agreed to be interviewed, but I did not have the resources for travel to his home in Tasmania. I did ask if he would be willing to come to the United States if I could secure his travel expenses. He agreed, so I asked Ms. Mead if she could find travel expenses for Douglas if I would make arrangements and conduct an in-depth interview over a two- or three-day period. It seemed like a good idea for everyone. I would get my material for the biography of Joy, Wheaton College would have the beginning of a C. S. Lewis oral history collection, and Douglas Gresham could fulfill his desire to put his recollections on tape, dispel some myths being promulgated about his mother and C. S. Lewis, and at the same time see the rich collection of primary and secondary sources pertaining to his famous stepfather.

Marjorie Mead eagerly embraced the idea. Somehow she found the funds, and Douglas Gresham and I went to Wheaton in 1982. The oral history interview required many hours spread over two days. Gresham's reminiscences became the core of his splendid book *Lenten Lands*, published in 1988.

During the several conversations with Marjorie Mead, I urged her to consider launching a major oral history project on C. S. Lewis before everyone who knew him well died. She acknowledged the importance of such an endeavor but pointed out that the founding director of the Wade Collection (its early name), Dr. Clyde S. Kilby, was about to retire and that the college had begun a search for his replacement. Mead said that despite the fact that Kilby's academic position was professor of English and therefore the search was on for someone in that discipline, perhaps it would be timely to hire a professional historian—especially one with training and experience in oral history research. She then offered the suggestion that caused me to make a career move that among other things paved the way for this book: "Why don't you apply for the position and do the oral history project yourself?" Long story short, I applied, was hired, departed the University of Denver, and became professor of history and director of the Wade Center at Wheaton College in 1983. In brief, without Marjorie Mead's prompting and her unflagging encouragement and support then and over the past twenty years, I never could have conducted scores of formal oral history interviews, carried on a number of "off-the-record" and informal conversations with other associates of Lewis, found Lewis's personal library, and generally basked in the primary source material absolutely essential to tell the story in this book.

Serving the Wade Center with a vision for an oral history project was one thing, but finding the time and money to travel extensively was something else. Once again Ms. Mead stepped forward. She agreed to supervise the Wade Center staff and oversee the day-to-day operations of this growing library and archive in order to free me for travel. Still, however, the problem of funds stood in the way. The Wade Center has a modest endowment, but fluctuating markets sorely restricted the budget for travel and acquisitions.

At this point God sent another angel-like helper. Professor Carol Kraft, at that time a faculty member at Wheaton College who taught German language and literature, sat on the Wade Center advisory board and frequently prayed with us as we all sought God's blessing and guidance for the Wade Collection's endeavors. To the point, Carol Kraft donated funds to cover the travel expenses. Her extraordinary generosity paid for numerous trips conducted in Britain from 1983 through 1989. She likewise offered constant prayer support and encouragement.

My wife, Mary—always my best friend, coworker, encourager, and critic—became an indispensable colleague on the oral history project. She ably operated the video camera and the audio backup. During interviews she frequently yet unobtrusively slipped me questions I would have overlooked. Like a coach on the sidelines, she gave me occasional hand signals to stop pushing a point or to go further and press a particular line of questions. Her charm, wit, and gift as a conversationalist melted more than one shield of ice—especially for people who say an interview is almost as intimidating as oral surgery, especially when conducted by an American professor with a full beard. Besides helping with interviews, Mary proved to be a superb navigator as we drove compact rental cars with stickshifts over thousands of kilometers annually throughout the United Kingdom. We made at least one and sometimes two or three trips a year for seven years. I simply could not have traversed all the back roads to the sometimes remote villages without Mary's encouragement and companionship. Also, she typed and offered an invaluable critique of this manuscript.

Besides these three people, I am indebted to the able staff at the Marion E. Wade Center. I especially thank Christopher Mitchell, the director, and the excellent staff that he and Marjorie Mead have overseen. The staff make the Wade Center one of the most comfortable and efficiently functional research facilities in the English-speaking world.

Three colleagues on the faculty at Wheaton College gave me encouragement as I pursued this and other projects related to C. S. Lewis: Wayne Martindale, Mark Noll, and Jerry Root.

Father Martin Smith, Society of St. John the Evangelist in Cambridge, Massachusetts, helped me understand spiritual direction in the SSJE tradition. He also contributed his book on Robert Meux Benson, and he generously arranged for Father A. E. Bean, SSJE, to correspond with me. Father Bean knew Father Walter Adams, Lewis's spiritual director, and proved to be an invaluable source.

Graduate research assistants who helped along the way are Tisha Cooper, Jake Hanson, Allison Hennessey, and Bob Henry. Allison and Jake, in particular, provided invaluable help during the final stages of preparation. In truth, I could never have met the publisher's deadlines without Jake Hanson's careful checking of all the documentation.

Over the course of seven years, I personally interviewed forty-two people. Only a half-dozen or so would not allow me to tape our conversation. The recorded interviews are all owned by the Wade Center. Among the people I want to single out are the late Owen Barfield, who granted numerous hours of formal interviews in 1983 and 1984. Then and for the next few years he politely submitted to brief follow-up visits that were not recorded. Indeed, some of my best conversations with him occurred when I drove him on errands. The informality of the car, the fresh air and open country, and the absence of the recording equipment elicited some of his most useful memories.

Douglas Gresham proved to be extremely helpful. Because of our common commitment to keeping the life and works of Lewis before the public, we have become good friends and he has always been supportive of my work.

George Sayer, author of *Jack: C. S. Lewis and His Times* (1988), not only granted several interviews in England and Wheaton, but he and his wife, Margaret, offered us gracious hospitality on several occasions.

The late Stephen Schofield, editor of *In Search of C. S. Lewis* (1984), gave me formal and informal interviews. He and his wife, Esther, invited us to stay in their home every time we visited England. On my first trip to do Lewis interviews, I was traveling without Mary. Esther fed me and packed a lunch (actually a small feast) so I would not get hungry on the road. Stephen reacted in horror when he saw I intended to travel the back roads of England with only a folded paper map. He maintained that I would never get around without a large, detailed map book of the United Kingdom. He went right out and bought one for me before I took to the road. He was right. I needed it. I've kept it and continue to use it.

Miss Jean Wakeman, one of the few close friends Joy Davidman found in England, granted an interview on Joy as well as subsequent interviews on Jack and Warnie Lewis. Her spirit, intelligence, charm, and hospitality will never be forgotten.

These are the generous souls—some no longer alive on this earth—who granted interviews: Owen Barfield, Pauline Baynes, Peter Bide, Harold H. A. Blair, Harry Blamires, B. B. Crighton-Miller, Howard Davidman, Maureen Moore (Lady Dunbar), Roger Lancelyn Green, Douglas Gresham, Alan Bede Griffiths, Robert E. "Humphrey" Havard, R. E. Head, Frank Henry, Clyde S. Kilby, Clifford Morris, Martin Moynihan, Monica Moynihan, Mary Neylan, Stephen Olford, Ruth Parker, Ruth Pitter, Barbara Reynolds, Luke Rigby, Mary Rogers, Val Rogers, George Sayer, Stephen Schofield, Kenneth Thompson, Alec Vidler, Jean Wakeman, Chad Walsh, Eva Walsh, Christopher L. Wiseman, Nicholas Wyatt, Alice Mary Hadfield, Charles Hadfield, Aiden Mackey, Kathleen Richards, Anne Ridler, and Ruth Spalding.

I am grateful to my friend Kenneth Tanner, who recommended this book to Rodney Clapp, editorial director of Brazos Press. I thank Rodney for his suggestions that certainly improved the final draft. Rebecca Cooper, managing editor, offered invaluable assistance.

I also thank Jim Bell, my friend and sometimes editor, who pushed me to get this book going. And I am grateful to Wheaton College for a sabbatical leave in 2003 to do the writing.

PREFACE

While I deeply admire C. S. Lewis the man, and although I have been profoundly blessed by his writing, I do not agree with everything he taught and proclaimed. Nevertheless, as a student of his life and writings for well over two decades, I have been intrigued by a question that has inspired this book: How did C. S. Lewis mature spiritually after his conversion to Christianity in 1931? He wrote—and so have others—about the process leading up to his conversion. But, despite the many books on Lewis, the biographers are not particularly helpful on this subject, and Lewis himself—except in largely unpublished letters—failed to tell us how he grew from infancy to maturity in the Christian faith.

Of course, we know that Mr. Lewis found nurture in prayer, Scripture, the church, and experience with other Christians. He also made it quite clear that a few authors, among them George MacDonald, George Herbert, and G. K. Chesterton, fed his heart and mind. My goal, however, is to go beyond these obvious and commonly recognized influences and get into the largely overlooked factors of his spiritual formation. In the following pages I attempt to explore the process of his spiritual maturation with particular emphasis on how his understanding and practice of prayer changed over the years. I also try to illumine his changing understanding and use of Scripture, as well as his changing views of the church and sacraments. Besides the authors he frequently mentioned and recommended, who were the theologians and clergy who had the greatest impact on his spiritual formation? How did their guidance help fashion Lewis's development as a disciple of Christ? I further maintain that Mr. Lewis imbibed what he learned and then became an informal yet markedly influential spiritual director to numerous people—some of them over a period of many years. Finally, this book is intended to cause the reader to ask, What is there that C. S. Lewis passed on to spiritually infirm or hungry souls that helps us today?

Finding some answers to these questions has enriched my understanding of C. S. Lewis. Through the preparation of this book my soul has been blessed and healed in several ways. Furthermore, I have been constrained to employ a few of Lewis's methods and recommend some of his prescriptions for the care of souls in my context of ministry. My prayer is that what I have found will strengthen and encourage you as you seek to walk more intimately with the Lord Jesus Christ.

1

INTRODUCTION

"God Grant Me to Say Things Helpful to Salvation"

To the casual observer, nothing in particular set C. S. Lewis apart from the crowd. When he described himself to some young admirers who had neither met him nor seen his picture, he could have been describing countless twentieth-century men: "I'm tall, fat, rather bald, red-faced, double-chinned, black-haired, have a deep voice, and wear glasses for reading."[1] If he had

---

1. C. S. Lewis to "Fifth Grader," May 29, 1954, in C. S. Lewis, *Letters to Children,* ed. Lyle W. Dorsett and Marjorie Lamp Mead (New York: Macmillan, 1985), 45. (C. S. Lewis hereafter referred to as CSL.)

gone on to describe his clothing, he would have admitted to paying scant attention to clothes, dressing in nothing similar to the fastidious likes of T. S. Eliot or those fashionably groomed entrepreneurs and professionals who frequented haunts such as London's Pall Mall Club. Indeed, except on rare occasions, Lewis's year-round attire consisted of trousers rounded at the knees—hinting that they might have been slept in; a tweed jacket pitted by tobacco burns—the telltale evidence of his chain-smoking habit with cigarettes and pipe; and shoes at once down at the heel and hungering for polish.

If C. S. Lewis's personal habits and wardrobe allowed him to blend into the crowd of ordinary mid-twentieth-century Englishmen, he manifested an unusual spiritual transformation after his genuine commitment to Jesus Christ in 1931. Although this Oxford-based academician enjoyed a splendidly rich and well-rounded life—filled with books, friends, fellowship, holidays, and hiking adventures—he nevertheless became a man with a single eye. From the early 1930s until his death three decades later, Lewis developed a passion to know Christ, obey him, and make him known. Furthermore, he became a spiritually magnetic man. From childhood and youth, to be sure, he modeled a remarkably alert mind. But after his middle thirties he gradually and unselfconsciously took on a magnetism that at once attracted numerous spiritual seekers and repulsed those who seemed hardened toward God.

Another Englishman, Frederick B. Meyer, a pastor and Bible teacher who ministered on both sides of the Atlantic in the late nineteenth and early twentieth centuries, offered an observation that helps explain C. S. Lewis's remarkable depth. Meyer told his friend Dwight L. Moody, America's most popular late-nineteenth-century evangelist, that "the Spirit of the Lord Jesus Christ is present in all true Christians. He is prominent in some, and He is pre-eminent, alas, in only a few." After Meyer experienced his own spiritual transformation, he became convinced that Christ called him to tell as many Christians as possible that Christ desires to be preeminent in each of them. Consequently, Meyer invited people who were stirred by such a possibility to try a few spiritual prescriptions guaranteed (from the promises of Scripture) to enable Christians to experience an increasingly Christlike transformation in their souls.

Although Mr. Lewis never knew Frederick B. Meyer, he did come to know and manifest the truth embodied in such teaching. Indeed, the Spirit of Christ certainly became preeminent in C. S. Lewis. And like the Baptist preacher Meyer of an earlier generation, Lewis, who employed a different rhetoric to be sure, pursued a markedly similar goal: to point people to Jesus Christ, show them ways they can know him deeply and intimately, and encourage them to become alluring souls who make him attractive to others.

For over a quarter of a century I have devoted considerable time to reading biographies and autobiographies of Christian men and women whose lives have touched many souls in ways that still bring great glory to God. The people I have encountered through books span many centuries and several continents. Their vocations, education, and social classes were markedly diverse, and their denominational and historical traditional affiliations covered a wide spectrum. Nevertheless, they did not worry about the breadth of their ministries. Instead they focused on the depth of their relationship with the Lord Jesus Christ, leaving the Holy Spirit to care for the breadth.

Few twentieth-century Christians in the English-speaking world have had a wider range of influence than C. S. Lewis. And like saints of earlier eras, he faithfully and purposively focused on the depth of his relationship with Christ Jesus, and the Holy Spirit has taken care of the breadth of his influence. That Mr. Lewis paid scant attention to his widespread fame, or had any real sense of his profound contribution to the rescue and care of souls, is evidenced by a terse response he made to his close friend and legal adviser, Owen Barfield. Not long before Lewis died, Mr. Barfield asked him how he planned to allocate the royalties of his books, which would surely be substantial after his death. Mr. Barfield told me that Lewis dismissed the issue by saying, "After I've been dead five years no one will read anything I've written."

My major goals in writing this book are first to explain how C. S. Lewis cultivated his ever-deepening relationship with Christ; and second, to suggest some ways, besides book sales, that the Holy Spirit, unbeknownst to Lewis, widened his breadth of influence.

After his conversion, C. S. Lewis embarked on an extraordinarily purposeful life. He became, as Dorothy L. Sayers phrased it, "God's terrier"—a man with "missionary zeal."[2] Nearly three decades after he became a follower of Christ, Lewis admitted that most of what he had written was "evangelistic."[3] By this he meant that his books were in one way or another designed to point people to Jesus Christ. Some works were crafted to point non-Christians to the Messiah, while others were written to help people young in the faith understand the basic

2. DLS to George Every, July 10, 1947, Sayers Collection, Wade Center, Wheaton College.

3. CSL, "Rejoinder to Dr Pittenger," *Christian Century* (November 26, 1958): 75.

tenets of Christianity, apply them, and thereby grow into mature disciples.

Born in Belfast, Northern Ireland, in 1898, Lewis converted to Christianity in 1931. By the time he died thirty-two years later, he had written nearly forty books and a long list of essays, articles, and poems. Educated and living most of his adult life in Oxford, England, C. S. Lewis nonetheless would have an influence that reaches all over the world. Most of his books are still in print, sales grow each year, and his books are translated into dozens of languages. For three-quarters of a century, this Oxford-educated scholar has been inspiring, edifying, and spurring on people of all ages. Over the two decades that I have been teaching and lecturing on C. S. Lewis and his wife, Joy Davidman, I have met hundreds of people who told me how Lewis's writing pointed them to Christ. Countless others have explained how Professor Lewis became their spiritual guide through his books when they could find no one else to help them. Some of our most influential Christian writers testify that this author assisted them onto the Calvary road, among them Charles Colson and Os Guinness. Similarly, a Presbyterian pastor, the Reverend Rodman Fridland, told me that in 1958 the Committee on Ecumenical Missions and Relations (COMAR) surveyed 415 missionaries in the United Presbyterian Church. Among other questions, they asked, "Who was the most influential person in your becoming a missionary?" Fifty percent of those on the mission field wrote "C. S. Lewis" on the questionnaire.

For years Lewis's extraordinary effectiveness in touching souls has intrigued me. After reading hundreds of his letters, studying his publications, examining his notes in his personal library, and interviewing dozens of people who knew him personally, it is obvious that he possessed an unusually keen mind that had been honed by a first-rate education. Beyond this, Lewis became a superb stylist. He wrote simple sentences and his prose is strikingly clear. He made skillful use of analogy, he encoded some of his messages in fascinating works of fiction, and he made able use of allegory and metaphor. Although it is apparent that many factors have conspired to make C. S. Lewis's writing so magnetic, I am convinced that nothing is more important than his deep spirituality. The words from his long-silenced pen still flow with unusual power because the author's talent, imagination, and inspiration sprang from an unusually dynamic relationship with Jesus Christ. In brief, his influence is wide because his personal spirituality was deep.

Lewis's deep spirituality did not emerge in a few months or even a few years after his conversion. On the contrary, like all Christians—even the greats like the apostle Paul and early fathers of the church—Lewis had to discipline both his mind and soul. He had to learn spiritual discipline and seek guidance on his spiritual pilgrimage, just like everyone else.

Numerous friends and acquaintances over the years have asked me what I have learned about Mr. Lewis's own spiritual formation beyond the several autobiographical works he wrote that focus primarily on his conversion and the death of his wife. In part, this book is an attempt to answer those questions. But it is also written because I personally have hungered to find the secrets to his spiritual development for myself. Indeed, in some respects this is a markedly personal book.

In my thirties, several people gave me books by C. S. Lewis. My reading of *Mere Christianity* and *Surprised by Joy* achieved what the donors intended—these books nudged me toward faith in the Lord Jesus Christ. Likewise, hearing my wife read the Narnian Chronicles to our children at breakfast caused a hunger for more knowledge of Christ and His kingdom. Then after I came to faith, C. S. Lewis became a teacher through several more of his books. He taught me about spiritual warfare in *The Screwtape Letters*, and *Letters to Malcolm: Chiefly on Prayer* answered many practical questions and offered a foundation for a theology of prayer. *The Problem of Pain*, *Miracles*, and several shorter pieces helped me explain to skeptical friends and acquaintances why I had become a Christian. And many of Lewis's published letters, especially some in *Letters to an American Lady* (edited by Clyde S. Kilby) and *Letters* (edited by Warren H. Lewis), became important guideposts in my spiritual formation.

Because Mr. Lewis's writing so profoundly influenced my spiritual development, there were many questions I would have asked him if we had met, but that could not be. He died in 1963—a dozen years before I began to read his books. I wished to ask my erstwhile mentor how he grew spiritually. In particular, I was curious about the spiritual disciplines he practiced and how he employed Scripture and prayer in his pilgrimage. I wondered, too, what writers most shaped his thinking about Christianity, and what people offered unusually helpful assistance to him along the way. In brief, I would have said, "Professor Lewis, what have been the foundational elements of your spiritual formation? Can you help me learn from what has encouraged you?"

Although C. S. Lewis "passed over into his own Country," as he once described the death of a Christian friend, he still left enough evidence behind to provide some solid answers to my questions. Thanks to Lewis's own autobiographical writings, especially *A Pilgrim's Regress* (1943), *Surprised by Joy* (1955), and *A Grief Observed* (1961), we have helpful glimpses of his inner life. Likewise, several important biographies shed light on this fascinating and complex man. Among the most useful are Chad Walsh's *C. S. Lewis: Apostle to the Skeptics* (1949), Roger Lancelyn Green and Walter Hooper, *C. S. Lewis: A Biography* (1974), William Griffin, *Clive Staples Lewis: A Dramatic Life* (1986), and *Jack: C. S. Lewis and His Time* (1988) by Lewis's friend and confidante, George Sayer. David C. Downing has written an excellent book on Lewis's conversion, titled *The Most Reluctant Convert* (2002). This is not a biography, but it is an excellent portrait of the man and his pilgrimage to faith. The biography by A. N. Wilson published in 1990 is so filled with factual errors and inaccurate interpretations that it is useless to the serious student of Lewis's life and writing.

The published biographical and autobiographical literature of this truly exceptional teacher and writer constitutes a rather clear picture of his inner life up to his conversion to Christianity in 1931. But the biographical literature covering the last three decades of his life is somewhat misleading, albeit not deliberately so. What emerges is a picture of man who converts to Christianity and then seemingly quickly becomes a mature Christian whose life is consumed with lecturing, tutoring, and writing a remarkable collection of books, essays, and poetry. The only time between 1931 and his death in 1963 when a fuller picture of Lewis emerges comes in his relationship with his wife, Helen Joy Davidman. This love story and Mr. Lewis's spiritual agony during Joy's battle with cancer and eventual death are covered in a biography of Joy Lewis, *A Love Observed*,[4] and in Lewis's own little volume *A Grief Observed*.

---

4. Lyle W. Dorsett, *And God Came In: The Extraordinary Story of Joy Davidman* (New York: MacMillan, 1983); revised and updated as *A Love Observed* (Wheaton: Harold Shaw Publishers, 1998); hereafter referred to as Dorsett, *And God Came In*.

No one, of course, is completely transformed at the time of conversion. If justification is immediate, spiritual maturity is a process that comes over time, even for someone as brilliant, well-educated, and clearly called and gifted by God as C. S. Lewis. This transformation into Christlikeness, holiness, or Christian maturity—whatever rhetoric one chooses to use—is realized in different ways by each person. But the rapidity and depth of the process is directly related to a person's willingness to cooperate with the Holy Spirit's guidance, and most certainly spiritual growth is nurtured or hindered by the quality of teaching and mentoring one finds.

To find answers to questions about Lewis's spiritual formation, I have spent considerable time over the last two decades collecting and studying a variety of primary sources. My wife, Mary, and I traveled the United Kingdom for several weeks each year during much of the 1980s. We interviewed over forty people who were relatives, friends, and associates of C. S. Lewis. On one trip, we discovered his personal library, which had found a temporary home in an out-of-the-way college in England two years after he died. In this collection of approximately 2,400 volumes (housed at the Marion E. Wade Center, Wheaton College, since 1985) are numerous volumes containing Lewis's own marginal and endpaper notes. Lewis's personal library reveals insights into his reactions to a large body of literature—some of it relating to spiritual formation.

Studying Lewis's unpublished letters and book annotations alongside oral history reminiscences of people who knew him has produced many answers to my questions about his spiritual formation. Along with these answers has come a fresh and more robust view of the man whose writings have helped shape the souls of countless Christians for nearly seven decades. Furthermore, it has been exciting and instructive to see C. S. Lewis of Oxford emerge in the august company of the apostle Paul, Clement of Rome, Catherine of Sienna, John of the Cross, Martin Luther, John Wesley, and a long list of other women and men who have nurtured souls through letters. Many people sought Lewis's counsel about the care of their souls. Because of limitations of time, distance, and personal preference (he was more comfortable writing than talking one-to-one about spirituality), Lewis willingly served as a soul physician and spiritual mentor to a considerable number of people through the mail. To some people he dispensed all that they required in two or three letters. For others he prayerfully and thoughtfully served as their spiritual director for much longer periods—in some cases over many years.

Perhaps because C. S. Lewis has been one of my important spiritual awakeners and teachers I have therefore been more doggedly determined than many Lewis scholars more talented than I to learn all that is available on how he grew spiritually. In any case, through the grace of God and the generous cooperation of many people, I have been able to pan the sands of some unsifted primary sources and garner a golden treasure.

The nuggets from this delightful enterprise have enriched my soul. Quite simply, my faith in Christ and understanding of Christian spirituality have grown significantly. Therefore I make the treasures I've found available to people who read C. S. Lewis and wish they could have him as a mentor or spiritual guide.

Perhaps I should be reticent to reveal my discoveries, particularly since Lewis made known his disdain for "inquisitive researchers" who, as he phrased it, "dig out all our affairs and besmirch them with the poison of 'publicity' (as a barbarous thing I am giving it a barbarous name)."[5] But I go ahead with this project because I know Lewis's deepest desire, to use his own words, was to "work—with a generous heart and with an intrepid faith for the spread of God's Kingdom." Indeed, Lewis's friend and biographer, George Sayer, told me that Lewis remarked that most of the letters he received from an admiring public contained questions about his personal and spiritual life. Mr. Lewis also confessed that he found the volume of correspondence to be quite burdensome, especially by the 1950s, when he would sometimes receive scores of letters every week. But Lewis also admitted that he believed the Lord had called him to answer each piece of fan mail with care, as a service unto Him. Sometimes when the mail was piled unusually high, he told the Lord that he would have time to write more books if there were fewer letters to write. Nevertheless, he practiced what he wrote to one girl: the important thing is to obey Jesus, even if you don't understand why He asks you to do it.[6] In fact, Mr. Lewis began a letter to one man with these matter-of-fact words: "I always answer fan mail."[7] Indeed, he intimated to a friend that sometimes our most important duty to God is doing seemingly small things such as respond to "the young man who seeks my advice" because there "the Lord Himself is present."[8]

As Mr. Lewis got on with the business of answering the mail—even when he didn't understand why the Lord required this rather burdensome task—he had no idea

5. CSL to Don Luigi Pedrollo, January 3, 1961, in Martin Moynihan, ed. and trans., *Letters, Don Giovanni Calabria: A Study in Friendship* (Ann Arbor: Servant Books, 1988), 103–5, hereafter referred to as Moynihan, *Letters*.

6. CSL to Sarah, April 3, 1949, in *Letters to Children*, 25–27.

7. CSL to Mr. McClain, March 7, 1945.

8. CSL to Don Giovanni Calabria, March 27, 1948, in Moynihan, *Letters*, 47.

that some of his most important books would be volumes of his letters, made up of the fruit of his obedience.

The portions of letters, the notations from books, and the gleanings from memories of Lewis's associates, I trust, will reveal nothing that should remain in sacred silence like a person's confession to a pastor or priest. Instead, the following pages are offered in the spirit that C. S. Lewis said he was in while preparing his book on the four loves: "Pray for me that God grant me to say things helpful to salvation, or at least not harmful."[9]

9. CSL to Don Luigi Pedrollo, March 28, 1959, in Moynihan, *Letters*, 101.

PRAYER

"Sustained and Regular Habit"

In the early 1950s an elated C. S. Lewis wrote to an American World War II veteran whose soul he had prayed for with much diligence. The two men had met in Oxford after the war when Sheldon Vanauken, an honest seeker after truth, had engaged Lewis in several discussions about the Christian faith. Their dialogue continued through the mail and came to a climax in April 1951. "My prayers have been answered," Lewis wrote, going on to warn the new convert that the enemy of our souls would launch "a counter attack on [him]." Do not be "alarmed" or confused, he told Vanauken, when it comes, because "the enemy will not see you vanish into God's company without an effort to reclaim you." His next move, Lewis urged, was to "be busy learning to pray."[1]

These five words—"be busy learning to pray"—encapsulate what Lewis assumed to be the most important advice he could pass on for the protection and nurture of this newly converted soul. Prayer is essential, he maintained, and you must be busily and diligently engaged because prayer is a discipline that must be learned through practice.

When he wrote to Vanauken, C. S. Lewis had been "busy learning to pray" for twenty years as a committed Christian. But his education in understanding this essential element in spiritual growth went back to early childhood. Born on November 29, 1898, on the edge of Belfast, Northern Ireland, he was baptized as an infant by his maternal grandfather, who was an evangelical pastor in the Church of Ireland.[2] Both Clive Staples (he renamed himself Jack as a child) and Warren Hamilton (nicknamed Warnie), his only sibling and his senior by three and a half years, were raised by Christian parents who faithfully prayed for them in an environment of Ulster Irish Protestantism. The immediate and extended family was thoroughly Calvinist in their theology and believed that the boys were "grafted" into the church through their infant baptisms. No doubt they prayed faithfully for Jack and Warnie's protection from evil and for their growth in the faith, as they vowed to do at the boys' baptisms.[3]

---

1. CSL to Sheldon Vanauken, April 17, 1951, quoted in Sheldon Vanauken, *A Severe Mercy,* Davy's Edition (San Francisco: Harper & Row, 1980), hereafter cited as Vanauken, *A Severe Mercy.*

2. A photocopy of Lewis's baptismal certificate and other documents related to early childhood are in the Wade Center.

3. Ruth James Cording, *C. S. Lewis: A Celebration of His Early Life* (Nashville: Broadman & Holman, 2000), and "Lewis Family Papers," in the Wade Center.

By the standards of both Ireland and the world, the Lewis boys grew up in markedly privileged circumstances. Their father, Albert James Lewis, maintained a prosperous legal practice in the environs of greater Belfast. Their mother, Florence Augusta Hamilton Lewis, was an attractive woman whose natural beauty was exceeded only by her brilliant mind. A stay-at-home mother, she loved her family and fostered an atmosphere in which her sons were encouraged to obey God, attend church, and be grateful for their advantages of going to school, reading widely, and generally basking in an environment that encouraged a love for books and pursuits of the mind.

Jack and Warnie enjoyed living in a large red-brick house named Little Lea. Not only did they have ample space inside for children's games of hide-and-seek, their lovely home was filled with books that they were encouraged to read and discuss. Beyond these considerable advantages, Little Lea was situated on spacious grounds where the boys could play outdoors and ride their bicycles on safe and remote suburban pathways and roads.[4] An environment sheltered from the dirt, smoke, noise, and congestion of growing Belfast—a city marked by pain and poverty—Little Lea provided comfort and a continuous supply of clean air.

Holidays at the seashore, family pets, and the companionship of relatives further enriched this idyllic world. Indeed, only Warnie's departure for college-preparatory school brought disruption to Jack's sheltered childhood. Certainly, young Jack had fallen under the illusion that prosperity, peace, and happiness were the evidence of God's love. He had not lived long enough to see how the

4. See CSL, *Surprised by Joy: The Shape of My Early Life* (New York: Harcourt, Brace & World, 1956), and George Sayer, *Jack: C. S. Lewis and His Times* (San Francisco: Harper & Row, 1988).

faithful often suffer, and from his sheltered suburban world he had not observed the abject poverty of many lovers of God who resided in the slums of nearby Belfast.

Just a few months before his tenth birthday, however, this veneer of prosperity theology began to warp. During the early months of 1908 Flora Lewis's activities were curtailed when she began experiencing severe abdominal pain. In February 1908 a surgeon removed a cancerous growth from her abdomen during a surgical procedure performed in her bedroom. Although Mrs. Lewis initially showed signs of recovery, her condition worsened in June. The warm and loving atmosphere at Little Lea gradually disappeared. By August nine-year-old Jack was frequently awakened from sleep at night by the troublesome sounds of people whispering and tiptoeing in and out of Flora's room.

Someone in the family urged the boys to pray for their mother's recovery, assuring them that if they prayed and trusted God, she would be healed. Throughout July and early August Jack and Warnie did pray. They confidently expected their mother to be healed because they had been assured of Jesus' very own promise that "whatever you ask in prayer, you will receive," if you have faith.[5]

Perhaps Flora Lewis prayed after Jesus' example in the Garden of Gethsemane, asking God to remove her cup of suffering and imminent death, but all the while seeking his will rather than her own. In any case the Lord soon made His will known. Realizing she would not escape death, and no doubt concerned about the spiritual well-being of her sons, she prayed for them and gave each lad a Bible as a parting gift.[6]

5. Matthew 21:22.
6. Warren Lewis related this to Clyde S. Kilby, the founder and first director of the Marion E. Wade Center at Wheaton College. Mr. Lewis also gave to the Wade Center the Bible his mother had inscribed and given to him.

Flora Lewis died August 23, several days after she prayed for her sons and signed their Bibles. A wise woman, she knew her death would shake their confidence in God. Nevertheless, she had faith that her prayers and the gifts of Holy Writ would somehow bring them through their personal crises.

Mrs. Lewis's prayers were answered, but not immediately. Both Warnie and Jack gradually turned from God in their despair. Not surprisingly, they were disappointed in God. Did He not hear their prayers? Did He care nothing for them and their mother? Was He a sadist who enjoyed inflicting pain? To them, God seemed indifferent, impotent, or mean.

Jack was sent off to boarding school after his mother's death. He did try to read his Bible, pray, and obey his conscience. But his personal world was devastated. He had horrid dreams that his father took his brother and went off to America, leaving him behind. He would awaken and offer up prayers of desperation, but his conscience told him that his prayers were not said properly.

If his father was schooled enough in prayer and sound theology to help Jack through this season of devastation, he made no apparent effort. Perhaps he, too, had a crisis of faith. In any case, he fell into a pit of depression and self-pity from which he never fully emerged. From Flora's death in 1908 until his own death in 1929, except on the most superficial levels, Albert Lewis became estranged from his sons. He remained a good provider, but could not muster the strength to be a teacher, friend, or encourager to his hurting boys.[7]

7. See CSL, *Surprised by Joy*, ch. 1, and W. H. Lewis, "Memoir of C. S. Lewis," in *Letters of C. S. Lewis*, ed. W. H. Lewis (London: Geoffrey Bles, 1966). (W. H. Lewis hereafter referred to as WHL.)

Finding no solid Christian guidance from their father, or anyone else for that matter, Jack and Warnie gradually slipped into pessimism. Their university experiences encouraged agnosticism and atheism. The carnage they personally saw in combat in World War I pulled them even farther away from the faith of their childhood.

Jack and Warnie Lewis remained aloof from the faith of their parents for about twenty years. Then, significantly, they both moved from their deistic if not atheistic worldviews almost simultaneously when their father died. Jack did not become an avowed Christian until 1931, but after his father's death in 1929, he did begin reading Brother Lawrence's *The Practice of the Presence of God*, George MacDonald's *Diary of an Old Soul*, and Thomas Traherne's *Centuries of Meditation*. He also began attending 8:00 a.m. chapel regularly at Magdalen College, and he cautiously entered into a habit of prayer.[8] On December 24, 1930, he wrote to his friend Arthur Greeves, reporting he had been reading novels of George MacDonald. He also wrote: "I think the trouble with me is lack of faith. I have no rational ground for going back on the arguments that convinced me of God's existence; but the irrational deadweight of my old skeptical habits, and the spirit of the age, and the cares of the day, steal away all my lively feelings of the truth; and often when I pray, I wonder if I am not posting letters to a non-existent address."[9]

8. William Griffin, *C. S. Lewis: A Dramatic Life*, 76–84. Warren Lewis wrote in his "Memoir of C. S. Lewis" that Jack was "reconverted" in 1931 (WHL, *Letters*, 19).

9. CSL to Arthur Greeves, December 24, 1930, in *They Stand Together: The Letters of C. S. Lewis to Arthur Greeves* (1914–1963), ed. Walter Hooper (London: Collins, 1979).

A few months later Lewis wrote to Greeves: "I have just passed on from believing in God to definitely believing in Christ—in Christianity—my long talk with [Hugo] Dyson and [J. R. R.] Tolkein had a great deal to do with it."[10]

Flora Lewis's prayers were answered. Nevertheless, for well over a quarter-century C. S. Lewis wrestled with what he called, in the title of one essay, "Petitionary Prayer: A Problem without an Answer." He observed that Christian teaching "seems at first sight to contain two different patterns of petitionary prayer which are inconsistent."[11] One pattern is the "actual prayer of the Lord in the Garden of Gethsemane ('if it be possible . . . nevertheless, not as I will but as Thou wilt')." The other pattern, he maintained, is in Mark 11:24: "Whatsoever you ask believing that you shall receive you shall obtain."[12] For years Lewis posed this question: "How is it possible for a man, at one and the same time, both to believe most fully that he will receive and to submit himself to the Will of God—Who perhaps is refusing him?" Lewis said he had searched the writings of the Doctors of the Church for help in solving his problem and found no answers. He also consulted numerous contemporary theologians and clergymen, who could not help him either.[13]

Only after spending years "learning to pray" did he conclude that some saints with special gifts and unusual closeness to the Lord supernaturally discerned that they are to ask God for what He purposed to do. Such prayers of faith, Lewis concluded, are "for very advanced pupils

10. CSL to Arthur Greeves, October 1, 1931, in Hooper, *They Stand Together*.

11. CSL, "Petitionary Prayer," in *Christian Reflections*, ed. Walter Hooper (Glasgow: Collins, 1983).

12. CSL to Fr. John of Calabria, January 1953, in Moynihan, *Letters*, 79.

13. Ibid., 79, 83.

indeed." Even as late as a few months before his death, he did not consider himself one of those "advanced pupils." On the contrary, this challenge in prayer to expect what you ask for, to Lewis's mind, was not addressed to men at his level of understanding and is "the worst possible place at which to begin Christian instruction in dealing with a child or Pagan."[14] Rather than citing the devastation that such well-meaning but hurtful teaching had wreaked on his own young life, Lewis instead pointed to Mark Twain's novel *Huckleberry Finn*: "You remember what happened when the Widow started Huck Finn off with the idea he could get what he wanted by praying for it. He tried the experiment and then, not unnaturally, never gave Christianity a second thought."[15]

As a mature Christian, C. S. Lewis looked back on his conversion in 1931 and saw himself as "the most reluctant convert in all England." What brought him back to the faith of his mother? Was it the mark of the covenant in baptism? The nurture of a Christian community during his childhood that he could never escape? The efficacy of a faithful mother's prayers? The persuasion of friends at Oxford in the 1920s and 1930s, or reading books of such men as G. K. Chesterton and George MacDonald? Perhaps all of these. In any case Lewis never really tried to explain the mystery of his conversion. He quite simply knew that the Holy Spirit put a longing in his heart and pursued him until he fully surrendered in the autumn of 1931. He knew his salvation was all grace. Although he called himself a reluctant convert,

14. CSL, *Letters to Malcolm: Chiefly on Prayer* (London: Geoffrey Bles, 1964), 83.
15. Ibid.

he never maintained his conversion was irresistible or that he was predestined and without a choice.[16]

Whatever combination of factors brought C. S. Lewis back into the Christian faith, one thing is certain: prayer became absolutely essential for him to keep that relationship with God strong. "The soul that has once been waked, or stung, or uplifted by the desire of God, will inevitably (I think) awake to the fear of losing Him." Lewis went on to say that prayer naturally flows from there. "What is more natural, and easier, if you believe in God, than to address Him?"[17]

If addressing God, whom he now acknowledged and worshiped, became natural and essential, just how this discipline of prayer should be practiced still had to be learned. When first entering the school of prayer after 1931, Lewis said he never used "ready-made forms except the Lord's Prayer." In fact, he recalled that he "tried to pray without words at all—not to verbalize the mental acts." His practice was to pray for others and not even mention their names. Instead he "substituted mental images of them." Perhaps this is a higher form of praying, he later conceded, but it required "greater mental and spiritual strength" than he possessed.[18] Later on Lewis realized that his prayers, if they were to be anything, must be real. "The prayer preceding all prayers is, 'May it be the real I who speaks. May it be the real Thou that I speak to.'"[19]

Lewis gradually laid aside all pretense, high-mindedness, and self-styled mysticism. Others could quite properly enter

16. See CSL, *Surprised by Joy*, and W. H. Lewis's "Memoir of C. S. Lewis," in WHL, *Letters*, especially 19. He stresses the gradualness of the "conversion." See also David C. Downing, *The Most Reluctant Convert* (Downers Grove, Ill.: InterVarsity Press, 2002).

17. CSL, *Letters to Malcolm*, 102–4.

18. Ibid., 20.

19. Ibid., 109.

into higher and more ethereal realms, but for him, as James Houston phrased it, "his spirituality" became "earthy, full of realism, for he was dead scared of sentimentalism. It was expressive of a no-nonsense kind of faith."[20] Consequently, Lewis's prayer life was soon guided by utmost practicality and based on what he found in Scripture and how that would play out in practice. In the Lord's Prayer, Jesus taught us to pray "Thy will be done." Initially, Lewis recalled, he saw that phrase as an exhortation to submit his will—however difficult. But he came to understand it as more. Rather than merely "Thy will be done," he came to see it also as "Thy will be done." In other words, we are to accept what befalls us, to be sure, but we are also to get on with what He has assigned us to do.[21]

Whereas some Christians liked to stress praise and thanksgiving as higher forms of prayer, implying if not teaching that petitionary prayer is for elementary students and should eventually be outgrown, Professor Lewis maintained that our Lord taught us to petition our Heavenly Father for our daily bread and to make all our requests known to Him.[22] He applied this down-to-earth practicality in others ways. He showed, for instance, that when we feel anxiety waiting for reports of doctors' tests or X-rays, we should not feel guilty if we wish we could hibernate or go underground. This is not a defect of faith, as we are tempted to believe. On the contrary, these anxieties "are afflictions, not sins. Like all afflictions, they are, if we can so take them, our share in the Passion of Christ." Our Lord in Gethsemane was in great agony. And the angels came and "strengthened"

20. James Houston, "The Prayer Life of C. S. Lewis," *Crux* 24, no. 1 (March 1988): 3.

21. CSL, *Letters to Malcolm*, 39–40.

22. Ibid., 72–73.

Him, as it says in the Greek, not "comforted" Him, as it is usually rendered in English.[23]

C. S. Lewis eventually developed a vigorous prayer life because he saw that our lives do in truth influence God. For instance, He forgives sins, but He would not need to do so if we had not sinned. "And if He takes our sins into account, why not our petitions?" In this vein he went on to say that we certainly influence God, or how else can we cause His wrath, pity, and grief?[24] Lewis tenaciously held to the belief that "one of the purposes for which God instituted prayer may have been to bear witness that the course of events is not governed like a state but created like a work of art to which every being makes its contribution (in prayer) a conscious contribution, and in which every being is both an end and a means."[25]

Joining into this artistic enterprise enthused C. S. Lewis throughout the years of his Christian pilgrimage. That we creatures are coworkers with the Creator quite simply excited him. He wrote that "creation seems to be delegation through and through. He will do nothing simply of Himself which can be done by creatures. I suppose this is because He is a giver. And He has nothing to give but Himself. And to give Himself is to do His deeds—in a sense, and on varying levels to be Himself—through the things He has made."[26]

Prayer was a meaningful privilege, to be sure, but that did not mean it was always a delightful activity. Lewis fully understood that we are created to love, worship, and enjoy God, but until we reach heaven we will not be in an environment of unimpeded obedience. On the

23. Ibid., 61–63.
24. Ibid., 72–73.
25. Ibid., 79.
26. Ibid., 95–96.

contrary, numerous things distract us. Therefore we must get on with our duty to pray, whether we feel joyful and enthusiastic or not.[27]

"Be busy" at prayer, he told Vanauken, and what he prescribed he certainly practiced. James M. Houston, who lived in Oxford and knew Lewis personally between 1946 and 1953, remembered that the Oxford don "never spoke about prayer." Quite to the point, "Lewis was never forthcoming about his own prayer life." There were no doubt many reasons for this reticence, but part of it lay in the simple truth that Lewis was shy. He "no more discussed religion too intimately" than you would talk "about your kidneys." Furthermore, Lewis had suffered much from the reactions of cynical Oxford colleagues who accused him of "dabbling" in theology when he was neither ordained nor a trained theologian.[28] On the other hand, Houston observed Lewis's lifestyle closely enough to say that there was a "practical rhythm" that he normally followed early each day during the academic terms. "He would rise about 7 a.m., take a walk, attend matins at 8 a.m. in College Chapel, and start tutorials at 9 a.m."[29]

From the time of his conversion Lewis became devoted to corporate worship and prayer. He saw community worship in one's particular church as indispensable to spiritual health and growth. In addition to maintaining his routine of regular worship at College Chapel, or Dean's Prayers as he called it, he felt constrained to attend his parish church on Sundays. When staying in his rooms at Magdalen College over weekends, he

27. Ibid., 145–48.
28. See Houston, "Prayer Life," 2. Also, Owen Barfield told me that Tolkien was upset that Lewis dedicated *The Screwtape Letters* (London: Collins, 1979) to him, because Jack had no business writing such a book since he was not trained in theology.
29. Ibid., 4.

would attend worship services at the Anglican convental church in the Retreat House of the Society of St. John the Evangelist, located just off the Cowley Road within walking distance of the college. Otherwise he attended the Anglican parish church at Headington Quarry, Holy Trinity, which lay within a short walk of The Kilns, the house he and Warren owned. In Lewis's mind it was unthinkable to search for a local church to find congenial companionship and a community of peers who shared a similar social and economic status. On the contrary, heaven will be filled with all sorts of people, so we need to worship God together now in preparation for the future. Thus, one should attend one's local parish, and not seek an alternative worship community. Lewis's parish church near The Kilns comprised a wide range of people—few indeed who had any sense of what transpired in his world of books, ideas, and students. Most of the parishioners at Headington were unaware or unimpressed by his renown in the world of popular theology. His parish priest recalled that few if any parishioners knew or cared that his picture adorned the cover of *Time* magazine in the United States during the first week of September 1947, let alone that some of his books were bestsellers translated into scores of languages and read by people all over the world.[30]

Personal or private prayer became increasingly woven into the fabric of C. S. Lewis's spiritual life. His correspondence reveals that the numbers of people he prayed for grew as his publications poured from the presses and reached an ever widening audience. His letters not only show that he offered up prayers for men,

30. See *The Screwtape Letters* for some of his views on community worship in the local church. Also, my interview with Fr. R. E. Head, Lewis's parish priest at Headington, was quite revealing about how the parish folk saw and interacted with Mr. Lewis. The oral history interview with Fr. Head is located at the Wade Center.

women, and children who lived throughout Britain, the Commonwealth countries, and the United States, but reveal his serious concern for their needs as well as his confidence that God would hear his prayers.[31]

This busy writer, lecturer, and tutor gradually extended his prayer times to early in the morning and late at night, but his best time for intercessory prayer was early evening.[32] He sometimes prayed, weather permitting, during late afternoon strolls through the Magdalen College grounds.[33] Lewis's private taxi driver, Clifford Morris, a devout evangelical Christian, told me that his frequent employer (Lewis never owned a car) was one of the most prayerful men he had ever known. He found Mr. Lewis to be warm and congenial, always treating him as an equal despite the wide disparity between their social classes and educational levels. This treatment surprised and blessed Morris, because other men—including Christians—were never so generous. Occasionally, Professor Lewis would get into the car and on the way to Cambridge say, "Morris, I'm sorry I can't talk for a quarter of an hour. I need to do my prayers."[34]

During busy times Lewis must have felt the prayers he promised to offer up for people were hardly a joy, but rather a burdensome duty. Nevertheless, as he told one of his correspondents, doing one's prayers albeit "grudgingly," "tho' a nuisance need not depress us too much. It is an act of will (perhaps strongest where there is some

31. See Lewis's *Letters to Children, Letters to an American Lady, Letters,* and Moynihan, *Letters,* as well as hundreds of unpublished letters in the Wade Center.

32. CSL to Miss Rhona M. Bodle, January 3, 1948, found in Bodleian Library, Oxford (hereafter cited as BL).

33. Houston, "Prayer Life," 4.

34. Oral history interview, Lyle W. Dorsett with Clifford Morris, May 27, 1986, Wade Center.

disinclination to contend against) that God values, rather than the state of our emotions—the act being what we give Him, the emotions what He gives us. . . ."[35]

Standing back and looking at Lewis's prayer life from the perspective of his correspondence reveals three striking patterns. First, he interceded faithfully for an unusually large number of people. And he took children and people he had never met just as seriously as his closer friends or people who had achieved some modicum of fame. Lewis, of course, as early as 1940 made it quite clear in print that "there are no ordinary people." Each soul is equally significant in the eternal scheme of things.[36]

A second pattern shows Lewis not only praying for others, but humbly seeking prayer for himself. Confident of his own need for prayer, as early as 1939 he wrote a letter to an Anglican nun, Sister Penelope, whom he held in high regard as a teacher and occasional spiritual guide: "Though I am forty years old, I'm only about twelve as a Christian, so it would be a maternal act if you found time to mention me in your prayers."[37] She did pray for him, and continued to do so for more than twenty years. "Pray for me," he typically begged her some years later. "I am suffering incessant temptations to uncharitable thoughts at present."[38] Besides those of Sr. Penelope, Lewis ardently sought the prayers of a host of others, including his brother, several American correspondents, two Catholic priests in Italy, and an Anglican monk in India.

35. CSL to Miss Rhona M. Bodle, January 3, 1948.

36. See his sermon "The Weight of Glory," published in *Theology*, November 1941, and reprinted in CSL, *The Weight of Glory and Other Addresses* (New York: Macmillan, 1949). See page 15.

37. CSL to Sister Penelope, July 9, 1939, in *Letters of C. S. Lewis*, ed. Walter Hooper (London: Collins, 1988), 321–23.

38. CSL to Sister Penelope, January 12, 1950, in Hooper, *Letters*, 222.

Examining Lewis's solicitations for prayer reveals a third pattern in the fabric of his prayer life—an international prayer network. C. S. Lewis, much like the apostle Paul two thousand years earlier, put together a prayer network that became truly multinational in scope. Lewis sought prayers for himself, his wife, Joy, during her battle with cancer, and his brother's occasional bouts with alcohol. He had people in North America, the United Kingdom, southern Europe, New Zealand, China, and the Indian subcontinent praying for these concerns and also for the conversion of lost souls for whom he was busily interceding.[39]

An inordinately busy academician, Professor Lewis had far too many demands on his time to spend so much of it praying, soliciting prayer, and encouraging others in this enterprise if he did not see prayer as an effective weapon against Satan and a powerful tool to build Christ's kingdom. Lewis became absolutely confident that petitionary prayer was "allowed," "commanded," and "efficacious." To be sure, this astute and devout layman had matured so as to understand that prayer is much more than petition. And he came to believe that petitionary prayer was not the loftiest kind of prayer we offer—certainly not always on the same plane as confession, penitence, and praise.[40] Nevertheless, he had been allowed to see many prayers answered. Warren's alcoholism never did conquer him,[41] Vanauken and many others became Christians, and perhaps most miraculous was Joy's story. Dr. R. E. "Humphrey" Havard, her personal physician, told me that Joy was hospitalized when her femur suddenly broke

39. See, for example, Lewis's letters in Moynihan, *Letters*, correspondence with Dom Bede Griffiths, R. Bodle, Van Deusen, and M. Shelborne.

40. See "The Efficacy of Prayer," *Atlantic Monthly* (January 1959): 59–61.

41. Oral history interview, Lyle W. Dorsett with Jean Wakeman, August 1, 1985, Wade Center.

while she was standing in her house. Upon examining her, he discovered her entire body (bones and most vital organs) was filled with cancer. Dr. Havard explained that he called Jack and told him the bad news and that he must prepare for her imminent death because she had only a few days—perhaps two weeks—to live.[42]

When Lewis heard the news he contacted his former pupil and friend, an Anglican priest, Peter Bide, whom Lewis knew to possess a gift of healing. Father Bide left his parish pastoral responsibilities in southern England, took the train up to Oxford, and prayed for Joy's healing at her hospital bedside. I talked to Father Bide in the 1980s, telling him I understood from others that he had a healing gift. He told me that "the Lord Jesus Christ sometimes chooses to heal people when I pray for them." He went on to say that the Lord apparently chose to place His healing touch on Joy Davidman Lewis, because she left that hospital a few days later to the utter astonishment of Dr. Havard and a host of other medical professionals. Joy Lewis not only left the hospital, she trampled through woods, even uphill in rugged terrain with Jack. She traveled to Ireland and Greece with Jack and made him a happy husband for nearly three more years.[43] What happened to Joy, given the advanced state of her cancer, was no common case of remission. God's timing and healing touch were clearly present.

Sometimes Lewis was like a child when he exuded excitement over answered prayer. "My prayers are answered" he celebrated when he learned Vanauken had become a believer. His delight over Joy's recovery

---

42. Oral history interview, Lyle W. Dorsett with Dr. R. E. "Humphrey" Havard, July 26, 1984, Wade Center.

43. Oral history interview, Lyle W. Dorsett with Fr. Peter Bide, July 1982, personal phone conversation. See also CSL, "The Efficacy of Prayer."

44. See Dorsett, *And God Came In*, as well as interviews with Havard, Bide, and George Sayer.

brought even more celebration.[44] His letter to Father John of Calabria brimmed with delight when he reported what seemed an answer to the Italian priest's prayers on his behalf. Lewis confessed that "it is astonishing that sometimes we believe what, really in our heart, we do not believe." He noted that for two decades he taught, wrote, and preached about forgiveness of sins, "but suddenly (on St. Mark's Day) this truth appeared in [his] mind in so clear a light that [he] perceived that never before had [he] believed it with [his] whole heart."[45]

One thing that truly delighted Lewis's soul—and it was a joy he frequently reiterated and attempted to pass on to others—was his coming to learn in the school of prayer that God invites us to be partakers in the execution of His will. "Can we believe that God ever really modifies His action in response to the suggestions of men?" In His infinite wisdom He certainly does not need us to tell Him what is best, and in His infinite goodness He does not need our urging to do His perfect will. "But neither does God need any of those things that are done by finite agents, whether living or inanimate." The philosopher in Lewis argued that God "could, if He chose, repair our bodies miraculously without food, or give us food without the aid of farmers, bakers, and butchers; or knowledge without the aid of learned men." God could convert all the heathens without missionaries, but "instead, He allows soils and weather and animals and the muscles, minds, and wills of men to co-operate in the execution of His will." He joined Pascal in maintaining that "God instituted prayer in order to lend to His creatures the dignity of causality."[46]

Five years before he died, C. S. Lewis, now well-schooled in prayer and a veteran from years of practice,

45. Moynihan, *Letters*, 67.
46. CSL, "The Efficacy of Prayer," 61.

observed that for himself petitionary prayer is "both allowed and commanded to us: 'Give us our daily bread.'" Nevertheless, "prayer in the sense of petition, asking for things, is a small part of it, confession and penitence are its threshold, adoration its sanctuary, the presence and vision and enjoyment of God its bread and wine. In it God shows Himself to us."[47]

The lesson to come last for C. S. Lewis in the school of prayer concerned praise. For him supplication came relatively early and the most easily, confession after much fear and trepidation (see ch. 4), and thanksgiving with increasing fervor each passing year. Praise, on the other hand, became the most difficult subject to grasp, even for this able and serious student of prayer. One of Lewis's last books, *Reflections on the Psalms* (1958), contains a chapter entitled "A Word about Praising." It could well be subtitled "Lewis and the Problem of Praise." In this splendid essay (ch. 9) Lewis candidly admitted, "When I first began to draw near to belief in God and even for some time after it had been given to me, I found a stumbling block in the demand so clamorously made by all religious people that we should 'praise' God." Refreshingly transparent about his own struggles, Lewis confessed that the Psalms troubled him because of the seemingly incessant exhortations to "praise the Lord" and "praise Him." People—and even whales—were urged to keep offering up praises. "Worse still was the statement put into God's own mouth, 'whoso offereth Me thanks and praise, he honoureth Me.'" To Lewis it seemed as if God said, "What I most want is to be told that I am good and great." He wrote that such an attitude disgusts us when we encounter it in humans.

Lewis also felt bothered by the evidence in Psalms that "mere quantity of praise seemed to count; 'seven

---

47. Ibid.

times a day do I praise thee'" (119:164). "It was extremely distressing. It made one think what one least wanted to think. Gratitude to God, reverence to Him, obedience to Him, I thought I could understand; not this perpetual eulogy." But after some years of gratitude, reverence, and obedience, the truth of God even "demanding" our praise came to light. It is not that God insists or demands our praises, it is that when we begin to see Him more clearly—then who He is demands one's praise. Gaining a clearer vision of Him simply awakens one to "the real world," and "not to appreciate" is to have lost the greatest experience, and in the end to have lost all.

Lewis excitedly recalled the delight of seeing "that it is in the process of being worshipped that God communicates His presence to men." To be sure this is not the only way He communicates his presence, "but for many people at many times the 'fair beauty of the Lord' is revealed chiefly or only while they worship Him together." For Lewis the wonder of praise of God became obvious when seeing that "the world rings with praise—lovers praising their mistresses, readers their favorite poet, walkers praising the countryside," and so on. Indeed, he finally noticed "how the humblest, and at the same time most balanced and capacious, minds, praised most, while the cranks, misfits and malcontents praised the least."[48]

It took Lewis several years to notice "that just as men spontaneously praise whatever they value, so they spontaneously urge us to join them in praising it: 'Isn't she lovely? Wasn't it glorious? Don't you think that magnificent?'" Therefore, it became evident what the psalmists did. By "telling everyone to praise God," they were "doing what all men do when they speak of what they care about."[49] Lewis finally realized that "we delight to praise what we

48. CSL, *Reflections on the Psalms* (London: Geoffrey Bles, 1958), 94.
49. Ibid., 95.

enjoy because the praise not merely expresses but completes the enjoyment; it is its appointed consummation." Indeed, "lovers keep on telling one another how beautiful they are" because "the delight is incomplete till it is expressed."[50] Therefore Lewis echoed John Donne and acknowledged that our praises might be imperfect and laden with questionable motives this side of Heaven, but we are "tuning our instruments. The tuning up of the orchestra can itself be delightful, but only to those who can in some measure, however little, anticipate the symphony."[51]

No soul-changing insights and practices were acquired immediately upon conversion or learned in a few months or years of becoming a serious disciple of the Lord Jesus Christ. Rather Lewis's rich knowledge of prayer and the God who ordains it grew out of a "sustained and regular habit of prayer," which emerged in large measure from his careful and practical study of Scripture.[52]

50. Ibid.
51. Ibid., 97.
52. Moynihan, *Letters*, 73.

3

SCRIPTURE

"Our Lord's Teaching Allows No Quarter"

As a mature Christian, C. S. Lewis wrote with confidence that God shows Himself to us in prayer, especially when we sing His praises. In the spirit of Psalm 22:3 this Oxford-educated intellectual maintained that exalting the Lord "is in reality indistinguishable from seeing Him."[1] These were by no means the utterances of a modern mystic, because Mr. Lewis more than once made it clear that he had little in the way of mystical

---

1. CSL to Firor, August 1949, BL.

faculty and saw only a few examples of mysticism in the New Testament.[2] Lewis's point was that he believed the Holy Spirit sometimes guides us from within when we pray "with the intention of pleasing God. The error would be to think that He speaks only within, whereas in reality He speaks through Scripture, the Church, Christian friends, books, etc."[3]

A writer and teacher who chose and ordered his words carefully, Mr. Lewis put "Scripture, the Church, Christian friends, books, etc." in this order by design. To him, these avenues of revelation were not equal. Scripture, to Lewis, is the place where we hear God most clearly and definitively. Scripture is the litmus test of the validity of all other sources of Divine guidance. When the church, a book, or a Christian friend instructs in a way contradictory to the plenary meaning of the Bible, C. S. Lewis firmly dismissed the other voices. For instance, because he believed that the Holy Spirit inspired the Scriptures, he pointedly responded to a woman who approached him with reservations about the doctrine of the virgin birth. Evidently some clergymen with whom she had discussed the topic denied the truth of Mary's virginity before the birth of Jesus. Lewis bluntly urged her not "to collect the opinions of individual clergymen, but . . . read Matthew and Luke I and II."[4]

In the same vein Lewis put Holy Writ above the institutional church if the teaching of the two happen to come into conflict. He cautioned one friend to "beware of the argument 'the Church gave the Bible and therefore the Bible can never give us grounds for criticizing the Church.'" He insisted that "it is perfectly possible to accept B on the authority of A and yet re-

2. CSL to Griffiths, September 1936, BL.
3. CSL to "A Lady," June 13, 1951, in WHL, *Letters*, 232–33.
4. Ibid.

gard B as a higher authority than A." Lewis says this is the case when he recommends a book to one of his pupils. "I first send him to the book, but having gone to it he knows (for I've told him) that the author knows more about the subject than I."[5] Likewise, if a highly acclaimed Christian writer should offer teaching that contradicted Scripture, his stand was the same. On one occasion, Lewis countered a friend who cited Pascal as an authority in a particular theological debate: "Yes," Lewis wrote, "Pascal does contradict several passages in Scripture and must be wrong."[6]

C. S. Lewis's eventual high view of Scripture might have been inspired by his mother's prayers when she gave him a Bible as a farewell gift in 1908, but if so he showed no evidence of it for over twenty years. In his early twenties he wrote in his journal that he had been in conversation with a fellow student at Oxford. They discussed Christianity and Lewis recorded his own observation that "one got very little definite teaching in the gospels." He admitted that the Gospel "writers had apparently seen something overwhelming, but been unable to reproduce it."[7] By the late 1920s Lewis was not even certain that the Gospel writers had seen anything at all. Indeed, by this time a serious student of pagan stories where gods visit the earth, he wrote of the incarnation as simply one more myth invented by the imaginations of men longing for a visitation from creatures greater than themselves.

5. CSL to "A Lady," December 28, 1961, in ibid., 302.
6. CSL to Dom Bede Griffiths, May 28, 1952, in Hooper, *Letters*, 422–23.
7. Journal of CSL, October 18, 1922, in WHL, *Letters*, 81–82.

"The Hound of Heaven" relentlessly pursued young Lewis at Oxford. By 1929, he had completed both the A.B. and a master's degree in classics, had lectured on philosophy for a year, and then had become a tutor and fellow in English language and literature at Magdalen College. All the while, however, his mind and his heart wrestled with the question of God's existence and goodness. Soon after his father died in 1929, part of the grieving process manifested itself in turning from atheism to theism. He occasionally attended the Anglican Church in Oxford, but carried persistent doubts about the literal truth of the Gospels. Jack Lewis's brother, Warren, made it clear in his "Memoir of C. S. Lewis," published in the mid-1960s, that his brother's autumn 1931 conversion to Christianity was "no sudden plunge into a new life, but rather a slow steady convalescence from a deep-seated spiritual illness of long standing—an illness that had its origins in our childhood. . . ."[8]

If the path to faith in Christ came gradually, there was an evening in September 1931 that was catalytic. Lewis excitedly conveyed the mystery and profundity of being birthed into faith in three letters that he wrote to his dear friend Arthur Greeves:

> He ["Hugo" Henry Victor Dyson, Inkling, and sometime extension lecturer at Oxford] stayed the night with me in College—I sleeping in in order to be able to talk far into the night. . . . Tolkien came too, and did not leave till 3 in the morning: and after seeing him out by the little postern on Magdalen bridge Dyson and I found still more to say to one another, strolling up and down the cloister of New Building, so that we did not get to bed till 4. It was really a memorable walk. We began (in Addison's walk just after dinner) on metaphor and myth—interrupted by a rush of wind which came so sud-

8. WHL, *Letters*, 19.

denly on the still, warm evening and sent so many leaves pattering down that we thought it was raining. We all held our breath, the other two appreciating the ecstasy of such a thing almost as you would. We continued (in my room) on Christianity: a good long satisfying talk in which I learned a lot: then discussed the difference between love and friendship—then finally drifted back to poetry and books.[9]

. . . I have just passed on from believing in God to definitely believing in Christ—in Christianity. I will try to explain this another time. My long night talk with Dyson and Tolkien had a good deal to do with it.[10]

From a letter dated October 18, 1931:

Now that Dyson and Tolkien showed me this: that if I met the idea of a sacrifice in a Pagan story I didn't mind at all: again, that if I met the idea of a god sacrificing himself to himself . . . I liked it very much and was mysteriously moved by it: again, that the idea of the dying and reviving god (Balder, Adonis, Bacchus) similarly moved me provided I met it anywhere except in the Gospels. The reason was that in Pagan stories I was prepared to feel the myth as profound and suggestive of meanings beyond my grasp tho' I could not say in cold prose "what it meant."

Now the story of Christ is simply a true myth: a myth working on us in the same way as the others, but with this tremendous difference that it really happened: and one must be content to accept it in the same way, remembering that it is God's myth where the others are men's myths: i.e. the Pagan stories are God expressing Himself through the minds of poets, using such images as He found there, while Christianity is God expressing

9. CSL to Arthur Greeves, September 22, 1931, in Hooper, *They Stand Together*, 421.

10. CSL to Arthur Greeves, October 1, 1931, in Hooper, *They Stand Together*, 425.

Himself through what we call "real things." Therefore it is true, not in the sense of being a "description" of God (that no finite mind could take in) but in the sense of being the way in which God chooses to (or can) appear to our faculties. The "doctrines" we get out of the true myth are of course less true: they are translations into our concepts and ideas of that wh. God has already expressed in a language more adequate, namely the actual incarnation, crucifixion, and resurrection.[11]

Soon after this memorable night Lewis announced to his brother, after a ride with him to the Whipsnade Zoo, that during the trip he was overcome by a great conviction: "When we set out I did not believe that Jesus Christ is the Son of God, and when we reached the zoo I did."[12] That was September 28, 1931. C. S. Lewis was two months from his thirty-third birthday. Standing squarely now in the middle of his life, he had made a complete surrender to the One who had haunted his mind and heart for years. He freely admitted that this was not merely an exchange of worldviews; it was a "new birth"—the beginning of redirection and revitalization of his whole person, spirit, soul, and body. For Lewis this was the onset of a "Transformation" into the likeness of Jesus Christ, whom he had so long doubted and then attempted to elude.[13]

In a pattern similar to that of many converts, C. S. Lewis developed a hunger for the Scriptures. Always a lover of books and student of the meaning of words,

11. CSL to Arthur Greeves, October 18, 1931, in Hooper, *They Stand Together*, 427–28.

12. CSL, *Surprised by Joy*, 237.

13. CSL, *Miracles* (New York: Macmillan, 1960), 172; appendix 11.

he purchased numerous Bibles and contrasted and compared the translations. I found more than a dozen Bibles that were still in his personal library over twenty years after his death, and several of these were in Greek. Because he read Greek almost as easily as he read English, he enjoyed evaluating the accuracy of new English translations by comparing them to the Greek texts he owned. He noted that Knox's translation is good literature but not as close to the Greek as Moffatt's. He argued in favor of accuracy of translation over the less essential aspects of style. He did, however, readily admit that one cannot be sure about the accuracy of newer translations without knowing well the Greek of the precise period a book was written. Finally, he mused that it is "odd, the way the less the Bible is read the more it is translated."[14]

If Lewis enhanced his Bible studies with Greek, he bemoaned his lack of Hebrew. In 1941 he confided to a friend that he envied her "Hebraic background," which enlightened her religious prose. And a decade and a half later, two years after marrying a Jewish woman, he published *Reflections on the Psalms*, admitting "I am no Hebraist" but that he still gained much from the Psalms, mainly by using Coverdale's translations employed in the Anglican Prayer Book.[15]

Although C. S. Lewis was an intellectual who lived in a world where ideas, books, and critical questioning were the order of the day, he by no means became like so many theologians, academicians, and pastors of his time who were, in the spirit of 2 Timothy 3:7, always learning and never coming to a knowledge of the truth. On the contrary, the Spirit seemed to so grip Lewis after

14. CSL to T. S. Eliot, May 25, 1962, in Hooper, *Letters*, 503–04.
15. CSL to Sister Penelope, April 10, 1941, in CSL, *Reflections on the Psalms*.

his conversion that he quickly and humbly went to the Holy Writ to hear it, feed upon it, and make practical applications to his everyday life. In 1943 he made his attitude quite clear in an article published in *The Guardian*. "Christians themselves," he argued, have brought upon themselves confusion about doctrine and biblical revelation. "They have a bad habit of talking as if revelation existed to gratify curiosity," whereas in truth, "revelation appears to me to be purely practical, to be addressed to the particular animal, Fallen Man, for the relief of his urgent necessities—not to the spirit of inquiry in man for the gratification of his liberal curiosity."[16]

Lewis became an increasingly diligent and practical student of the Bible. Already by the late 1930s and early 1940s, he was invited to preach, especially after *The Pilgrim's Regress* (1933) and *The Problem of Pain* (1940) were published. Then, with his radio broadcasts over the BBC during World War II that were devoted to a clear explanation of what was later published as *Mere Christianity*, he became much in demand as a visiting preacher and speaker to British Royal Air Force personnel. His driving ambition in these presentations was to translate basic Christian doctrine and biblical truth into a language ordinary laypersons could understand. Owen Barfield told me that his friend Jack Lewis received much criticism for his preaching, teaching, and writing on Christian topics. Indeed, J. R. R. Tolkien was embarrassed that *The Screwtape Letters* were dedicated to him. When I inquired why, Barfield said that Tolkien and others, including himself, felt that Jack, being neither a theologian nor an ordained clergyman, had no business communicating these subjects to the public.[17]

16. CSL, "Dogma and the Universe," *Guardian* (March 19, 1943): 26.
17. See my interviews with Owen Barfield in the Wade Center.

Mr. Lewis was well aware of the opinions of his critics, some of whom assailed him for his "Fundamentalist" stand on miracles and the teachings of Christ, while others chided him for making no original contributions to knowledge. To be sure, these derogatory criticisms caused the Oxford don emotional pain, but he went on with his ever growing sense of calling to communicate Christian truth so that people could understand it. His clearest explanation (not defense, because he never felt a need to defend his calling) of his writing came in "Rejoinder to Dr Pittenger," a liberal American theologian who found Lewis's writing "vulgar." Lewis wrote:

> When I began, Christianity came before the great mass of my unbelieving fellow-countrymen either in the highly emotional form offered by revivalists or in the unintelligible language of highly cultured clergymen. Most men were reached by neither. My task was therefore simply that of translator—one turning Christian doctrine, or what he believed to be such, into the vernacular, into the language that unscholarly people would attend to and could understand. For this purpose a style more guarded, more nuancé, finelier shaded, more rich in fruitful ambiguities—in fact, a style more like Dr Pittenger's own—would have been worse than useless.[18]

Lewis continued his rejoinder by admitting that he was a learner and if Pittenger or anyone else could help him communicate with his fellow countrymen more effectively, he would like to know what they do. He concluded, however, that one thing is certain. "If the real theologians had tackled the laborious work of translation about a hundred years ago, when they began to lose touch with

18. CSL, "Rejoinder to Dr Pittenger," *Christian Century* 75 (November 26, 1958): 1360.

the people (for whom Christ died) there would have been no place for me."[19]

The importance of a practical understanding and application of the Bible and doctrine was largely lost by the middle of the twentieth century. Therefore, Lewis urged those who administer ordination exams in the United Kingdom and the United States to take measures to correct this problem. "An essential part of the ordination exams ought to be a passage from some recognized theological work set for translation into vulgar English. . . . Failure on this paper should mean failure on the whole exam." Lewis concluded his recommendation by saying that "any fool can write learned language." With the following words the embattled writer closed his case: "The vernacular is the real test. If you can't turn your faith into it, then either you don't understand it or you don't believe it."[20]

Lewis both understood and believed biblical truth. And while it is true that he was neither ordained nor academically trained as a theologian, he in fact had gained considerable knowledge, albeit from self-education, in theology. His personal library reveals unusually wide and careful reading. For instance, less than five years after his conversion he devoured Gustav Aulén's *Christus Victor*. The volume is replete with his penciled underlinings and occasional question marks. Of course he read much more than what survived in his personal library. But even the remnant of this collection reveals careful reading of a wide range of theology, biography, church history, and biblical criticism. He consumed Richard Baxter's *Saint's Everlasting Rest*, plus several titles by John Bunyan. Besides these Calvinists, he read from a more Arminian perspective as well. He read and

19. *Christian Century* (November 26, 1958): 1360.
20. *Christian Century* (December 31, 1958): 1515.

annotated many works, among them writings of John Wesley and John Fletcher. Always eclectic in his reading, Lewis read sermons by John Cardinal Newman and Frederick Robertson. He also combed Martin Luther's *Table Talks* with care. He read several books on church history, including works on the Tudor and Stuart periods, with particular emphasis on Anglican history. He marked up his copy of A. O. J. Cockshut's *Anglican Attitudes*. And while no copy of Richard Hooker's works survives in his library, he often urged people to read Hooker's *Law of Ecclesiastical Polity* as the classical statement on what became the Anglican position. Lewis read G. W. Bromiley's *Biblical Criticism* and C. H. Dodd's *The Authority of the Bible*, as well as the scholarly theological works of his friend Austin Farrer. He dipped into the works of mystics such as Evelyn Underhill and Fenelon (in French), and his reading in Christian biography included François Mauriac's *Life of Jesus* and Bruno S. James's *Saint Bernard of Clairvaux*, as well as G. K. Chesterton's portraits *St. Francis of Assisi* and *St. Thomas Aquinas*, and even Maisie Ward's biography of G. K. Chesterton, an author who always remained one of Lewis's favorites.

In brief, C. S. Lewis became increasingly in demand to speak on Christian doctrine and biblical truth. Likewise, his book sales climbed with each passing year. His success in reaching an ever widening audience proved that the English-speaking public hungered for clear and intelligent material on the Christian faith. The man who fed them, unlike many theologians and pastors, could communicate clearly in the vernacular. And if this communicator was neither ordained nor trained in schools of theology, he was no ignoramus who tried to swim in waters way over his head.

Mr. Lewis's keen ability to translate Scripture into the vernacular grew from a regular and sustained habit of studying the Bible for personal transformation. Convinced that every soul is on a path toward Christlikeness or toward horrid corruption, he became convinced that imbibing Holy Writ was a primary source of spiritual nourishment for the disciple of Jesus Christ.[21] He not only drank in large drafts of Scripture daily, he insisted that the entire counsel of the Bible—all sixty-six books—was important for the health of his soul.

Like all public figures, Lewis was subject to scrutiny. And it is accurate to say that his love for God's Word did not please all regiments in the army of the faithful. The liberal element found his insistence that the entire Bible is "inspired" to be naïve and intellectually unsophisticated. To insist, as Lewis did, that the Gospels, Acts, and Epistles are historically accurate and that the authors wrote under the Spirit's guidance and protection was irresponsibly "Fundamentalistic." Ironically, the Fundamentalists found Lewis equally suspect. While he embraced the historicity of the Gospels—including the Virgin Birth and the physical resurrection of Christ Jesus, as well as other recorded miracles such as the turning of water into wine and the raising of Lazarus—he did not assume all of the Old Testament to be scientifically and historically accurate. For instance, Lewis argued, like Augustine before him, that the Hebrew canon contains several genres of literature. To his mind the Old Testament contains stories and poetry that are inspired but neither historic nor scientific. He did not assume the historicity of Jonah, Job, and Esther. From his vantage point as a serious student of literature, he maintained

21. See, for example, Lewis's sermon "The Weight of Glory."

that these are stories (fiction) that were given by the Holy Spirit to teach us just as surely as if they were events that actually happened. He believed that the Holy Spirit inspired the entire Bible in its overall message and that He speaks to us as profoundly through story and poetry (e.g., Song of Solomon and some Psalms) as He does through history.[22]

If one is to understand how Scripture transformed Lewis's mind, it is essential to know that he openly acknowledged that there is mystery in the Bible and that not everything is easy to understand. Lewis reminded people that even the apostle Peter admitted some of Paul's letters are difficult to understand. Furthermore, Lewis objected to the efforts of some systematizers and literalists who want to answer questions—for instance, what is life like after death? He also frowned upon attempts of some systematic theologians who attempt to explain mysteries that God simply has not revealed in Holy Writ.[23] "One of my main efforts as a teacher," he wrote to a man in Japan, "has been to train people to say those (apparently difficult) words 'we don't know.'"[24]

The confidence that kept driving Lewis back to the Scriptures with expectation to be fed and guided grew from his complete trust that the text is inspired and that

22. For his view of Scripture, see CSL to Clyde Kilby, May 7, 1959; to "A Lady," November 8, 1952; and to Mrs. Emily McLay, August 3, 1953. Extremely helpful are David Lyle Jeffrey, "C. S. Lewis, the Bible, and Its Literary Critics," *Christianity and Literature* 50.1 (autumn 2000), 95–110. And the most thorough and detailed study of this subject is Michel Christensen, *C. S. Lewis on Scripture* (Waco: Word, 1979). Although this book is nearly a quarter of a century old, it is still the standard work on this topic. See also Lewis's *Reflections on the Psalms* and ch. 7 in John Randolf Willis, *Pleasures Forevermore: The Theology of C. S. Lewis* (Chicago: Loyola University Press, 1983).

23. CSL to Emily McLay, August 3, 1953, in Hooper, *Letters*, 432–34; to Clyde Kilby, May 7, 1959, in Hooper, *Letters*, 479–80; to Vera Gebbert, October 16, 1960, in Hooper, *Letters*, 495.

24. CSL to Father Peter Milward, September 26, 1960, in Hooper, *Letters*, 494.

the Holy Spirit will answer honest questions and grant us what we need. There comes a time, he insisted, to "suspend . . . disbelief" and go to the Book simply "to feed on it."[25]

This is precisely what Lewis did, and he did it on a regular basis. He normally read daily from the Anglican Book of Common Prayer, steeping himself in the Psalms. In fact, following the book's pattern, he read the daily office, and he most likely read through all 150 Psalms each month. During the academic term he also went to morning prayer, or Dean's Prayers, at 8:00 a.m. at Magdalen College. There he heard more Scripture read in this brief service of worship, meditation, and prayer. As frequently as possible he also liked to set aside time in the late afternoon, preferably around 5:00 p.m., when he could read other parts of his Bible and pray. George Sayer, who offered Lewis hospitality annually so that two of them could hike the mountains of Malvern together, told me that Lewis almost invariably followed this pattern: After a good day's hike and tea, he would ask for a Bible if he had left his at home. Then he would retire to the guest room and pace up and down for about an hour, praying through portions of Scripture, often the Psalms.

The consistency of this behavior is confirmed after seeing the results of Arthur Rupprecht's research on the Latin letters Lewis wrote to two priests in Italy. Rupprecht shows how Lewis wrote the letters, regretting that he did not have a Latin New Testament at hand. Therefore, he apologized that he must express the sense of the Scriptures he cited in his own words. Lewis's Latin was beautiful and letter-perfect, but even more fascinating was the fact that his own wording for the Scriptures, albeit in Latin, revealed "a prodigious

25. CSL to "A Lady," November 5, 1952; *Reflections on the Psalms*, 7, 19.

memory of the King James Version of the Bible." In brief, by the late 1940s it is evident that C. S. Lewis had virtually memorized many portions of the English Bible in the King James Version.[26]

Whether or not Professor Lewis purposively devoted time to Scripture memorization is difficult to say. No solid evidence exists one way or another. But this man with an almost photographic memory never forgot long passages of poetry and prose that he had not read for years, so it is not surprising that he had a verbatim grasp of Scripture that he often read and reread. Suffice it to say, Lewis spent much time reading and meditating upon the Scriptures, and this was frequently done during his times of prayer. George Sayer said he prayed over Scripture every day in his home, even while on holiday. And when an American journalist interviewed Lewis six months before his death, one of his questions was, "What is your view of the daily discipline of the Christian life—the need for taking time to be alone with God?" Lewis responded, using Matthew 6:5–6 as his authority:

> We have our New Testament regimental orders upon the subject. I would take it for granted that everyone who becomes a Christian would undertake this practice. It is enjoined upon us by Our Lord; and since they are His commands, I believe in following them. It is always just possible that Jesus Christ meant what He said when He told us to seek the secret place and close the door.[27]

26. Arthur Rupprecht, "The Versatile C. S. Lewis: Latin Scholar," *Seven: An Anglo-American Literary Review* 18 (2001): 73–92. I also used a working paper he provided on this topic.

27. See Sherwood Wirt's interview with Lewis, published in two parts in *Decision*, September 1963 and October 1963. The interview took place in England on May 7, 1963.

For C. S. Lewis, daily routine of prayer and Scripture reading was not a yoke of legalism. It was simply obedience to the king we claim to serve. To obey Jesus is the doorway to intimacy with him as he was intimate with the Father. Lewis admits that sometimes God seems "real to [him]" and other times not. "It varies."[28] But the important thing is to obey Jesus whether we feel like it or not because "our Lord's teaching allows no quarter." Jesus might give us the feelings we "would like to have or not." But they do not matter. "The things that are happening to you are quite real things whether you feel as you [would] wish or not."[29]

As C. S. Lewis increasingly filled his mind with Scripture and then saturated it in prayer, his soul gradually became transformed into Christlikeness. Of course he would have been the first to confess his own sinfulness and flaws. Indeed, he made it clear that the more a person is transformed by Christ into His likeness, the more that person sees his sinful disposition.[30] Nevertheless, Lewis's attention to the depth of his ministry manifested itself in numerous ways. Obviously, the more he devoted himself to Scripture and prayer, the more he wrote. Furthermore, the impact of his writing was and continues to be phenomenal. Twenty years ago I placed some notices in several Christian magazines, asking readers to inform me if any of Lewis's writings had moved them toward faith in Jesus Christ. People's responses made up a folder full of fascinating letters[31] showing that everything from *A Pilgrim's Regress* to *The Screwtape Letters* constituted important signposts for people as they made their way to faith in Christ. Similarly, as I have spoken on C. S.

28. CSL to "Mrs. Ashton," July 17, 1953, in Hooper, *Letters*, 431–32.
29. CSL, *Reflections on the Psalms*, 19; CSL to Sarah (a goddaughter), April 3, 1949, in Hooper, *Letters*, 390–91.
30. CSL, *Mere Christianity* (New York: Macmillan, 1956), part 4, 149.
31. This file is housed in the Wade Center, Wheaton College.

Lewis in churches, colleges, and a wide assortment of conferences in the United States, Canada, Britain, and Ireland, I have frequently asked people to raise their hands if Lewis's works were instrumental in their becoming Christians. At almost every gathering several people raised their hands. Then when I say, "How many of you have been greatly assisted on your Christian walk by Lewis's writing?" even more hands go up.

Certainly such effects can never be quantified, but informal polls like these are an indication of the profound way God has used this man. One thing, however, is apparent. The more Lewis prayed and steeped himself in the Bible, the more God shaped his spirit and soul to do the work He had prepared him to do. Some of that work consisted of public speaking as well as writing books, articles, and essays for publication. Much of it, though, was writing letters to people who had read his books and wrote to him seeking spiritual counsel. Lewis's responses were increasingly filled with references to Scripture—especially quotations and paraphrases of the words of the Master. In brief, the more C. S. Lewis imbibed the words of the Lord, the more scriptural wisdom flowed from his pen to the minds and hearts of those who sought his advice. No wonder, then, that the piles of his letters that have survived are as timely today as they were when he wrote them.

4

THE CHURCH

"The New Testament Knows Nothing of Solitary Religion"

After his conversion to the Christian faith, C. S. Lewis always celebrated being a "mere" Christian. He loathed sectarianism and politics in the church. He desired to see Christians unite with one another over the essentials of the faith. And he devoted much of his writing to explaining basic doctrines and to encouraging people to follow Jesus Christ and live out His commands. In his preface to *Mere Christianity*—a work that has been widely read and celebrated by Christians from numerous traditions—Lewis makes it clear that in this work he offers "no help to anyone who is hesitating between two Christian 'denominations.' You will not learn from me whether you ought to become an Anglican, a Methodist, a Presbyterian, or a Roman Catholic." He emphasized that his purposes did not include "trying to convert anyone to [his own Anglican] position. "Instead," he said, "I have thought that the best, perhaps the only, service I could do for my unbelieving neighbours was to explain and defend the belief that has been common to nearly all Christians at all times."[1] To Lewis's mind the questions that divide Christians should be left to the experts in theology and church history. Let them debate among themselves and within their own communions. The discussions of disputed points, as valid as these are, should not be our primary concern. "So long as we write and talk about them," he argued, "we are much more likely to deter [the outsider] from entering any Christian communion than to draw him into our own."[2]

Lewis made it perfectly clear that he did not present "mere" Christianity "as an alternative to the creeds of the existing communions—as if a man could adopt it in preference to Congregationalism or Greek Orthodoxy or anything else." On the contrary, what he put forward "is more like a hall out of which doors open into special rooms." Lewis stressed that his purpose in writing *Mere Christianity*—a goal that in fact inspired most of his writing—was to bring people into the hall. But once there they must choose one of the rooms to enter, because "it is in the rooms, not in the hall, that there are fires and chairs and meals. The hall is a place to wait in, a place from which to try the various doors, not a place to live in."[3] In a lecture titled "Membership," he maintained

1. CSL, "Preface," *Mere Christianity*, v–vi.
2. Ibid., vi.
3. Ibid., xi.

that "the New Testament knows nothing of solitary religion." We must get into a church. "We are forbidden to neglect that assembling of ourselves together." He argued that "Christianity is already institutional in its earliest documents. The Church is the Bride of Christ. We are members of one another." Indeed, the modern cultural exhortation to keep religion as a private matter is unbiblical and at core un-Christian.[4]

Mr. Lewis never tried to hide the name of the "room" he entered through the grand hall of "mere" Christianity. Regarding his own beliefs, he wrote in the preface to *Mere Christianity* that "there is no secret. . . .They are written in the Common–Prayer Book. . . . I am a very ordinary layman of the Church of England, not especially 'high,' nor especially 'low,' nor especially anything else." Although he never attempted to recruit people for his Anglican domicile, he never hid his address or the reasons why his particular residency provided the nurture he needed to grow into Christlikeness. His high regard for his tradition comes out most clearly in a posthumously published book he finished just before he died, *Letters to Malcolm: Chiefly on Prayer*, and in many letters he wrote over a period of thirty years after his conversion.

To be sure, C. S. Lewis's spirituality was nurtured by prayer and Holy Scripture, but there is no way to understand the growth and strength of this great twentieth-century soul without seeing him in the caring hands of his spiritual mother, the Anglican Church. But to say he was Anglican in the three decades from his conversion in

4. "Membership," *Sobornost*, no. 31 (June 1945), reprinted in CSL, *The Weight of Glory* (Grand Rapids: Eerdmans, 1965).

1931 to his death in 1963 does not of itself reveal much. In the middle years of the twentieth century, Anglicanism was extremely diverse and in the midst of powerful pressures to change. To label Lewis an Anglican means little more than labeling him a Protestant. In Lewis's time Anglicanism ranged across a wide spectrum from "High Church" on one end and "Low Church" on the other. Although the High Church leaned closer to Roman Catholicism and the Low Church closer to a lower-church Protestant tradition somewhat similar to Methodism, all Anglicans stood on a system of doctrine and worship (including liturgy and sacraments) based on the Church of England's Book of Common Prayer. The 1662 edition, which was in Lewis's time still the official service book of the Anglican communion, was originally written by Thomas Cranmer and first published in 1549.[5]

Most Anglicans, whether high or low, stood on four sources of authority: Scripture, tradition, reason, and experience. The faithful orthodox Anglicans saw Scripture as the base of a quadrilateral, with tradition, reason, and experience standing on the Bible. The three upper parts are authoritative only if they withstand the test of biblical truth. Throughout the history of Anglicanism there have been factions that treated these sources of authority as an equilateral rather than a quadrilateral. And it is from this position that a "Broad Church"—indeed a liberal church—emerged that always advocated dialogue and frequently compromised with the spirit of the times. In Lewis's mind these "modernists" had given up orthodoxy in the name of being more inclusive and enjoying the contemporary culture.

C. S. Lewis insisted he was a "mere" Christian who lived in the room of orthodox Anglicanism. He con-

---

5. An excellent history of Anglicanism is Stephen Neill, *Anglicanism* (London: Penguin, 1958).

demned neither high nor low traditions within his communion, finding much good, as well as earnest commitment to the essentials of Christianity, across this wide spectrum.[6] Certainly, he was sometimes critical of the staunch Calvinists who influenced the low end of the Anglican continuum, despite his high regard of some sixteenth-century Puritans in his *English Literature in the Sixteenth Century, Excluding Drama* (1954). Lewis knew that the Calvinists were orthodox; therefore, he had no quarrel with them over essentials of the faith. What did bother him, however, was what he called the seventeenth-century Puritan objection to perfectly good practices. For instance, objections to drinking alcohol caused many people and eventually entire denominations to take up the "tyrannic and unscriptural insolence" of making "teetotalism" a mark of sincere Christians.[7] But even more disconcerting to Lewis was the Calvinist Reformed emphasis asserting predestination over free will, which he argued was "a meaningless question" that to his mind was "indiscussible, insoluable."[8] In his volume in the *Oxford History of English Literature*, Lewis strenuously objected to what he found in the writings of Thomas Cartwright, whom he described as a humorless man with a hatred for Catholics. Lewis also argued that the Puritan strain of Reformers manifested hypocrisy when they railed against the title "priest" for a pastor. The Puritan argument, according to Lewis, was that people must be left alone with God. Yet these same "Reformers" refused to trust people on their own. Many Puritans argued that we can hear God

6. See Lionel Adey, "How Far Did Lewis Change over Time?" *Canadian C. S. Lewis Journal*, no. 93 (spring 1998).

7. CSL to "A Lady," March 16, 1955, in WHL, *Letters*, 262.

8. CSL to "A Lady," October 20, 1952, in WHL, *Letters*, 245–46. See also Lewis's notes in his copy of the prayer book on this doctrine. Note on Article 13: "doctrine never to be discussed . . ." Wade Center, Wheaton College.

only through preachers, while the women in Bunyan's *Pilgrim's Progress* who are entrusted to Goodheart have been reproved for not having a "conductor." And while he recommended John Bunyan's *Pilgrim's Progress* as a good "mouth-wash for the imagination," you have to "ignore some straw-splitting dialogues on Calvinist theology and concentrate on the story [which is] first class."[9]

Another place where the Calvinists and Puritans rubbed against the grain of Lewis's spirit regarded the sinfulness that constantly lurks inside the converted man's soul. Clifford Morris, Lewis's driver, who faithfully drove him between Oxford and Cambridge on numerous occasions, told me that he urged Professor Lewis to read Alexander Whyte's book *Thirteen Appreciations*. Morris recalled that Lewis was not too keen on this evangelical's work. But if *Letters to Malcolm* is autobiographical (and Owen Barfield insisted that it is), then Lewis took issue with only one part of it. "I've been reading Alexander Whyte. Morris lent him to me. He was a Presbyterian divine of the last century, whom I'd never heard of." Lewis went on to say that he is "very well worth reading, and strongly broad-minded—Dante, Pascal, and even Newman, are among his heroes." The sole point with which Lewis took issue: "[Whyte] brought me face to face with a characteristic of Puritanism which I had almost forgotten. For him, one essential symptom of the regenerate life is a permanent, and permanently horrified perception of one's natural and (it seems) unalterable corruption. The true Christian's nostril is to be continually attentive to the inner cess-pool." It was this focus that bothered Lewis in *Grace Abounding* by

9. CSL, *English Literature in the Sixteenth Century, Excluding Drama* (Oxford: Oxford University Press, 1954), 441–51. CSL to Mrs. Margaret Gray, May 9, 1961, in WHL, *Letters*, 298–99.

the Calvinist John Bunyan, as well as in several authors quoted by historian William Haller in *The Rise of Puritanism*.[10] Lewis's personal and well-marked two-volume copy of Richard Baxter's *Saint's Everlasting Rest* elicited these endpaper jottings: "God have mercy on me if I am wrong, but I think this is a dreadfully misleading book" insofar as it relates to a feeling of assurance of salvation.[11] Lewis wrote that if he were a Calvinist, he would be full of "despair" over the fact that he did not always enjoy God. Indeed, sometimes my prayers feel like "a burden."[12] Lewis preferred to understand his feelings as undulations in the normal spiritual life and not necessarily as manifestations of unconfessed and unrepented sin.[13]

Clearly C. S. Lewis lived most comfortably in the Wesleyan and Arminian strain of Anglicanism rather than in the Calvinistic and Reformed domain embraced by such men as J. C. Ryle. This is particularly evident in his sermon "The Weight of Glory" delivered at the Anglican Church of St. Mary the Virgin in Oxford on June 8, 1941. It is also apparent in many of his books, among them *The Screwtape Letters* (especially letters 2 and 8) and *Letters to Malcolm*, plus numerous personal letters as well as evidence from his personal library, including John Wesley's *Journals*.[14] Like the ordained Anglican Mr. Wesley, Lewis had a powerful, heartwarming experience when he finally knew in his heart rather than just in his head that his sins were forgiven.[15] Also in the holiness tradition of John Wesley and his hymn-writing brother

---

10. CSL, *Letters to Malcolm*, 127–28.
11. See Lewis's copy in the Wade Center.
12. CSL, *Letters to Malcolm*, 146.
13. See CSL, *Screwtape Letters*, letter 8.
14. See John Wesley's *Journals* in Lewis's Library, Wade Center.
15. CSL to Don Giovanni Calabria, December 26, 1951, in Moynihan, *Letters*, 69–70.

Charles, C. S. Lewis believed that Christians should resolutely use their will through freedom in Christ to grow toward holiness, even though they will not fully attain it in this life.[16]

C. S. Lewis certainly stood in company that was uncomfortable with some of the doctrinal views of the Reformed wing of Anglicanism, but it would be wrong to conclude that he cared enough about these issues to engage in public debate. On the contrary, his theological position was not primarily presented in an offensive or aggressive way; rather, it is evident by inferences through his publications, for instance, in his celebration of Richard Hooker, Jeremy Taylor, and George Herbert in *English Literature in the Sixteenth Century*. It is in his letters where he most pointedly answers the questions of his correspondents, that he more overtly reveals a theological position antithetical to the Calvinists'. Indeed, Lewis never wanted to attack these fellow Anglicans, because he believed that these areas of disagreement were over secondary issues and not over essentials of the faith. Nevertheless, his love for the theological writings of Hooker and Taylor shows his closer identification with post-Reformation Anglican theologians who established their identity by finding a middle ground between the pre-Reformation church and the anti-Roman Catholic sentiments of the English nationalists and continental Reformers.

Mr. Lewis's attitude toward the modernists, on the other hand, was quite a different matter. Whereas he and the Reformed folks seldom spent time badgering

16. See D. E. Myers, "The Compleat Anglican: Spiritual Style in the Chronicles of Narnia," *Anglican Theological Review* 66, no. 2 (April 1984): 149.

one another, this was not the case with the modernists. In 1951 he wrote to a Roman Catholic friend with whom he disagreed over several major theological points (the Virgin Mary and the authority of the Magisterium, for instance), telling him, "I really think in our days it is the 'undogmatic' and 'liberal' people who call themselves Christians that are the most arrogant and intolerant. I expect justice and even courtesy from many Atheists and, much more, from your people [but] from modernists I have to take bitterness and rancour as a matter of course."[17]

Lewis took plenty of hits from the ever growing post–World War II liberal camp. As mentioned earlier, the Reverend Dr. W. Norman Pittenger, an American high churchman, went after Lewis in print. And many of the faculty at Oxford took verbal jabs at him as well.[18] Lewis could be equally combative with modernists, because to his mind many of them were not among the sanctified company of "mere" Christians. He maintained that some modernists led people away from orthodoxy and therefore from Christ and the truth, because, among other things, they refused to embrace miracles and the supernatural. In a lecture to Anglican ordinands he set forth the logic and evidence behind his rejection of "modern theology and biblical criticism" of such increasingly fashionable moderns as Rudolf Bultmann, Paul Tillich, Walter Lock, and James Drummond. Lewis expressed his thoughtfully-arrived-at disdain for the effects of modernism when it became manifested in sermons such as one by Alec Vidler, "The Sign at Cana." For Lewis's part, he found it "quite incredible

17. CSL to "A Lady," April 1, 1952, in WHL, *Letters*, 239–40.
18. Sheldon Vanauken related a story to me about men he overheard at Oxford. See *A Severe Mercy* (New York: Harper & Row, 1977), and see also CSL, "Rejoinder to Dr Pittenger," *Christian Century* 75, no. 26 (1958).

that we should have to wait nearly 2,000 years to be told by a theologian called Vidler that what the Church has always regarded as a miracle [changing water to wine] was, in fact, a parable!"[19] In the same vein Lewis argued that evangelical and Anglo-Catholics are united in a war against liberals and modernists, because they are, although rather different in some ways, "thoroughgoing supernaturalists, who believe in the Creation, the Fall, the Incarnation, the Resurrection, the Second Coming, and the Four Last Things. This unites them not only with one another, but with the Christian religion as understood *ubique et ab omnibus* [everywhere and by all]." He went on to say that those who maintain that the divisions between "High" and "Low" church are more important than this significant basis of agreement are, to him, "unintelligible." He says the "trouble is that as supernaturalists, whether 'Low' or 'High' Church, thus taken together, they lack a name. May I suggest 'Deep Church'; or, if that fails in humility, Baxter's 'mere Christians'?"[20]

For the most part, C. S. Lewis spent little time studying, analyzing, or criticizing the factions in the Anglican Church. Instead, he behaved like a member of a good family—giving what he could to encourage others and taking what was offered to him. He lived in the church and loved it, and from it he drew much of his spiritual vitality. Being in the church was to Lewis as important to healthy spiritual development as being in a family is

19. See "Fern-seed and Elephants," in CSL, *Christian Reflections*. See also my personal interview with Alec Vidler at his home in Rye, England, in 1986, where we discussed this sermon, which was critiqued by Lewis. Vidler's sermon was published in *Windsor Sermons* (London: SCM, 1958).
20. CSL, "Mere Christians," *Church Times*, February 8, 1952.

to emotional and social health. "The Christian is called, not to individualism," he insisted, "but to membership in the mystical body." But in this body we are not members of a social class where everyone is included in a homogeneous group. No. Christians are members of a body and therefore similar to organs—"things essentially different from, and complementary to, one another: things not only in structure and function but also in dignity." He found the illustration of the family helpful too: In a club or a social class, people who are regarded as members are "merely units." But "how true membership in a body differs from inclusion in a collective may be seen in the structure of a family." He illustrated it this way: "The grandfather, the parents, the grown-up son, the child, the dog, and the cat are true members (in the organic sense) precisely because they are not members or units of a homogeneous class. They are not interchangeable," Lewis insisted. "Each person is almost a species in himself. The mother is not simply a different person from the daughter, she is a different kind of person," and so forth.[21]

In the church Christ is the undisputed head of the body—a body we enter into through baptism. "The Head of this Body is so unlike the inferior members that they share no predicate with him save by analogy." We are called "to combine as creatures with our Creator, as mortals with immortal, as redeemed sinners with sinless Redeemer. His presence, the interaction between Him and us, must always be the overwhelmingly dominant factor in the life we are to lead within the Body." Lewis stressed that "any conception of Christian fellowship which does not mean primarily fellowship with Him is out of court." From there he moved to conclude: "After that it seems almost trivial to trace further down the diversity of opera-

---

21. CSL, "Membership," in *Weight of Glory*, 34.

tions to the unity of the Spirit. But it is very plainly there. There are priests divided from laity, catechumens divided from those who are in full fellowship." As unpopular as the concept was among the growing egalitarians, he further laid out that "there is authority of husbands over wives and parents over children. There is, in forms too subtle for official embodiment, a continual interchange of complementary ministrations."[22]

Offering up his gift of writing and teaching to church body and family, he wrapped up his point this way:

> We are all constantly teaching and learning, forgiving and being forgiven, representing Christ to man when we intercede, and man to Christ when others intercede for us. The sacrifice of selfish privacy which is daily demanded of us is daily repaid a hundredfold in the true growth of personality which the life of the Body encourages. Those who are members of one another become as diverse as the hand and the ear. That is why the worldlings are so monotonously alike compared with the almost fantastic variety of the saints. *Obedience is the road to freedom, humility the road to pleasure, unity the road to personality*[23] [italics are mine].

Mr. Lewis complemented the others in the church by giving what he could, including his tithe, praying for people, and maintaining a full schedule of teaching, preaching, and writing. During World War II he lectured on the faith over radio, and during the 1940s and early 1950s he did occasional preaching in several parish churches in Oxford. He also provided lectures on issues and doctrines of the faith to Anglican schools and monasteries, all the while producing a continuous stream of books, essays, and articles.

22. Ibid., 35–36.
23. Ibid., 36.

Elaboration on C. S. Lewis's contributions to the local and extended church is the focus of the next chapter. But first it is essential to see some of the significant ways the Anglican church shaped and nurtured his soul and thereby helped him fulfill his calling to the Anglican Christians in particular and all Christians in general.

The Anglican Church is part of the sacramental tradition of the historical Christian faith. Breaking from Rome in 1533, the Anglican Reformers rejected much that they believed had become corrupted and unbiblical in the larger Roman Catholic church. Besides dropping their allegiance to the pope and the magisterium, Anglicans adopted the Thirty-nine Articles of Religion that set forth their statement of faith and practice. The Anglicans removed the Apocrypha from the Canon of Holy Writ, relegating those fourteen books to a place of being useful as "example for life and instruction of manners" but not "to establish any doctrine." The Articles of Religion abolished the doctrine of Purgatory as well as worship and adoration of the elements of Holy Communion, relics of saints, and the practice of invocation of saints in prayer. Among other changes, the Anglicans officially recognized only two of the seven sacraments practiced by the Roman Church, these being Holy Communion and baptism, because they were both specifically ordained of Christ.

The Anglicans made a significant shift from Rome in the way they viewed Holy Communion. They rejected transubstantiation "or the change of the substance of Bread and Wine" into the actual body and blood of Christ. They further maintained that the bread should not, after the celebration of the Eucharist, be "carried about, lifted up, or worshipped." These changes expressed in the Articles of Religion notwithstanding, the Anglicans clung to a very high view of Holy Communion. Consequently, they embraced a doctrine wherein the Eucharist was much more than an ordinance and a memorial service; it was also a sacrament where the body and blood of Christ, through Christ's Spirit, are truly present in the bread and wine. Christ's Spirit, or "Real Presence," comes to the church in Holy Communion by grace through faith.[24]

In the Anglican Church, Holy Communion has always been central to public worship, and most of the faithful communicants see it as one of the most important ways to feed the soul. C. S. Lewis, however, did not have such a lofty view of either public worship or the Eucharist when he returned to the church in the early 1930s. His brother, Warren, recognized the importance of public worship and receiving Holy Communion, but in his "Memoir of C. S. Lewis" he remembered that this was not a comfortable posture for him and his brother. Major Lewis confessed that their childhood origins were filled with "the dry husks of religion offered by the semi-political church-going of Ulster, in the similar dull emptiness of compulsory Church during our school days." Not surprisingly then, "with this background, [they] both found the difficulty of the Christian life to lie in public worship, rather than in one's private devotions.[25] Outliving his brother by nearly ten years, in the mid-1960s Warren remembered that Jack took a rather limited view of Holy Communion in the 1930s. Warren wrote that Jack "had been a practicing Christian again for some time when he said to me of Communion: 'I think that

24. Richard Hooker promulgated the concept of "Real Presence" in the late 1500s. His view was embraced by most Anglicans, including C. S. Lewis, who admired his writings and recommended them to others.
25. WHL, "Memoir," in WHL, *Letters*, 19.

to communicate once a month strikes the right balance between enthusiasm and Laodiceanism.'"[26]

If C. S. Lewis needed several years to learn how to pray, he also needed time to grasp the importance of Holy Communion for growth and sustenance of his soul. Indeed, Warren wrote that "in later years [Jack] saw the 'right balance' differently, and never failed to communicate weekly and on major feast days as well."[27] Jack Lewis's former pupil and eventual close friend George Sayer remembered Lewis's transformation in a similar way. Sayer recalled that "at first" he took Communion only on "great holidays," but soon received the sacrament once a month. Sayer goes on to say that Lewis did not receive the sacrament weekly until "the last fifteen or so years of his life."[28]

The truth is that C. S. Lewis started regularly receiving Holy Communion at least once a week by the early 1940s, because his correspondence documents this marked change. During World War II, for example, he wrote to one correspondent: "Be sure your Communions are frequent and regular."[29] And it is inconceivable that once he began meeting regularly, in October 1940, with the man who for the next twelve years became his spiritual director that he did not become at least a weekly communicant. Throughout the 1940s and 1950s Lewis, to use the words of his longtime friend, Alan Bede Griffiths, increasingly acquired "a deep reverence for and understanding of the mystery of the Eucharist."[30]

26. Ibid.
27. Ibid.
28. George Sayer, *Jack*, 135.
29. CSL to Miss Gladding, June 7, 1945.
30. Quoted in an excellent article by Nancy-Lou Patterson, "Trained Habit: The Spirituality of C. S. Lewis," *Canadian C. S. Lewis Journal* 87 (Spring 1995): 47.

Lewis's awe of Holy Communion is expressed in *Letters to Malcolm*, a book Owen Barfield insisted must be seen as autobiography, in these words: "I find no difficulty in believing that the veil between the worlds, nowhere else (for me) so opaque to the intellect, is nowhere else so thin and permeable to divine operation. Here a hand from the hidden country touches not only my soul but my body."[31] Always honest about his limited understanding of things beyond his grasp, Lewis admitted that the spiritual reality of what takes place in the Eucharist is a mystery. Therefore, he expressed gratitude that our Lord Jesus Christ said "Take, eat, not Take, understand."[32]

No wonder then that Jack's close Roman Catholic friend J. R. R. Tolkien could find him a bit enigmatic. Writing to his son Christopher in 1944, Tolkien pointed out that despite the "good deal of Ulster still left in C. S. L. if hidden from himself," manifested in strong anti-Catholic prejudices, he "reveres the Blessed Sacrament and admires nuns!"[33]

31. CSL, *Letters to Malcolm*, 133.
32. Ibid., 136.
33. Humphrey Carpenter, ed., *The Letters of J.R.R. Tolkien* (Boston: Houghton Mifflin, 1981), 95, 96.

5

SPIRITUAL FRIENDS AND GUIDANCE

"A Wonderful Opportunity"

The master key to opening the secrets of C. S. Lewis's spiritual formation is his humility. Beginning in summer 1940, this gifted writer, teacher, and intellect fell under conviction that he needed a spiritual director. Such a decision came only after an agonizing season of prayer, because as James Houston observed, Lewis found it no more natural and easy to talk about his deepest spiritual concerns than to discuss his body parts. Always the academician and intellectual, Mr. Lewis loved to discuss books and ideas, but when it came to deep personal matters, he usually hid behind a cloak of privacy.[1] It is true that Lewis wrote an autobiography, *Surprised by Joy*, but it did not appear in print for nearly a quarter-century after his conversion, and it covered his life only up to that momentous event of 1931. To be sure he wrote *A Grief Observed*, an autobiographical meditation on his spiritual struggles surrounding his wife's battle with cancer and death. But this originally appeared in print under the pseudonym N. W. Clerk, to protect Lewis's privacy. And while *Letters to Malcolm: Chiefly on Prayer* is clearly autobiographical, it is auto-biography disguised as letters, and it appeared in print only after his death.

Reticence notwithstanding, Lewis submitted to the Holy Spirit's prompting, laid aside personal preference, and set out to find a man who would hold him account-able to confess his sins and repent. Such a man needed to be more than a good listener; Lewis wanted an expe-rienced physician of souls who towered above him in spiritual maturity, Christlikeness, and understanding of the deeper things of God. Lewis found the man and went to him in October 1940. A few days before his initial appointment, he wrote to a good friend and Anglican nun, Sister Penelope: "I am going to my first confession next week, wh[ich] will seem odd to you, but I wasn't brought up to that kind of thing. It's an odd experience. The decision to do so was one of the hardest I have ever made: but now I am committed (by dint of posting the letter before I had time to change my mind) I begin to be afraid of the opposite extreme—afraid that I am merely indulging in an orgy of Egoism." He acknowledged that although it "will be terrifying" to face, "it is a wonder-ful opportunity. Remember that resistance at the time

---

1. Houston, "Prayer Life."

means v[ery] little. Those who resist most violently in words are often those who go away and think it over most fruitfully."[2]

Lewis survived his first meeting. He wrote to Sister Penelope: "Well—we have come through the wall of fire and find ourselves (somewhat to our surprise) still alive and even well." He revealed that his concern about "an orgy of Egoism turns out, like all enemy propaganda, to have just a grain of truth in it, but I have no doubt that the proper method of dealing with that is to continue to practice, as I intend to do."[3] Good to his word, Lewis continued "to practice" for the rest of his life.

Lewis described Father Walter Frederick Adams as his "confessor and . . . Father in Christ," and "a man of ripe spiritual wisdom—noble minded but of an almost childlike simplicity and innocence."[4] Adams became what C. S. Lewis titled his director. To Lewis's mind a Christian who is purposive about growing in the faith must live a life of "self-examination, repentance and restitution," taking regular "Communion . . . and then to continue as well as you can, praying as well as you can . . . and fulfilling your daily duties as well as you can." Going further, "if one wants anything more e.g. Confession and Absolution which our church [Anglican] enjoins on no-one but leaves free to all," is not about going to a psychoanalyst. Rather, "the confessor is the representative of our Lord and declares His forgiveness." This director also gives "his advice or 'understanding'" of what is happening with your soul. And while this is of "real importance," it is secondary to the role of

2. CSL to Sister Penelope, October 24, 1940, BL.
3. CSL to Sister Penelope, November 4, 1940, BL.
4. CSL to Don Giovanni Calabria, April 14, 1952, in Moynihan, *Letters*, 71–72.

hearing confession and holding one accountable for repentance.[5]

It is doubtful that anyone had a more profound impact on Lewis's spiritual development in the spiritually formative years from 1940 to 1952 than Father Walter Adams. Seventy-one years old when he and Lewis first met, Adams was born in England in 1869. Walter's father served as an Anglican priest and encouraged his son to attend Keble College, Oxford. After his Keble years, Adams did further study at Wells Theological College. Then, in 1897, after ordination to the Anglican priesthood, he served as curate in two parish churches. In 1916, already in his forties and unmarried, Father Adams heard a call to leave parish ministry and become a mission priest of the Society of St. John the Evangelist.[6]

Adams's call was deemed by the Society of St. John the Evangelist (SSJE) to be from God, because the SSJE Rule states that "we whom God calls into this Society have been drawn into union with Christ by the power of his cross and resurrection; we have been reborn in him by water and the Spirit," and called "to make lifelong vows of poverty, celibacy and obedience in an enduring fellowship. . . ."[7]

The members of SSJE were commonly called the Cowley Fathers, because the Mother House was originally located off the Cowley Road on Marston Street at the edge of Oxford. The order's founder, Richard Meux Benson (1824–1915) became, according to some church historians, one of the most powerful and influential spiritual forces in late-nineteenth-century Anglicanism. A disciple of E. B. Pusey and a graduate of John Wesley's alma mater, Christ Church, Oxford, Benson

---

5. CSL to "A Lady," January 4, 1941, in WHL, *Letters*, 191–92.
6. *The Cowley Evangelist*, April 1952, obituary of Walter Frederick Adams.
7. Chapter 1, *SSJE Rule*.

became Vicar of Cowley. From this base he founded the SSJE in 1866—the first Anglican religious community for men. Unusually energetic and gifted, Benson served simultaneously as a parish priest, evangelist, and spiritual director. While he wrote nearly thirty books and became a leader in urban evangelism, he also pioneered the Anglican retreat movement."[8]

Although Benson died a year before Adams was received into the Society, Adams of course became steeped in Benson's teachings and fully imbibed the atmosphere of the SSJE. Benson's teachings and theological presuppositions were embraced by Walter Adams and therefore became part of the spiritual fare Lewis would have consumed as he learned from Adams and read his and Benson's publications. Lewis owned, read with care, and marked up a copy of Benson's work on the resurrection and ascension of Jesus Christ, entitled *The Life beyond the Grave*. And even a casual reading of Benson's writings and two little books by Adams reveals how much Lewis took from them and passed on to others in his own books and letters of pastoral care.

Benson had a passion for holiness, and he longed to know and love God more intimately. Influenced by the Oxford Movement, he exhibited a complete confidence in the Bible. He also drew much from the writings of Richard Hooker and Lancelot Andrews, and from them he gained a love for the pre-sixth-century church fathers. Benson's purpose in the SSJE was to train up missioner priests who shared his vision for unity of the spiritual, intellectual, and practical in Christian life, firmly rooted in a worshiping community that actively engaged in evangelism and spiritual direction. Benson and those

---

8. See Martin L. Smith, ed., *Benson of Cowley* (New York: Oxford University Press, 1900), and M. V. Woodgare, *Father Benson: Founder of the Cowley Fathers* (London: Geoffrey Bles, 1953).

he trained were encouraged to flee from what he saw as the intellectual aridity of scholastic Calvinism and post-Tridentine Roman Catholicism. A Christian mystic, Benson continually stressed the importance of the resurrection rather than staying limited to a focus on the cross. The ascended Christ became a reality to Benson. Indeed, when he practiced evangelism, offered spiritual direction, and led retreats, he proclaimed that the risen Christ is with us now. Members of the SSJE were expected to "truly seek God"—the One who still says "Come unto Me." This was the core of their calling. Like Stephen in Acts 7, the SSJE believed and made it a vocation to help others see and echo Stephen in saying, "I saw heaven opened and Jesus standing at the right hand of God." Benson wrote: "Alas, that we should ever pray without seeking to realize the fullness of that martyr's vision."[9]

Benson was extremely critical of the expression of the doctrine of apostolic succession when it maintained that a now absent Christ handed supernatural power over to the church. The idea that the church can minister through apostolic succession without a "really present" Christ here and now became unthinkable to him. One of Benson's ablest biographers, A. M. Allchin, wrote that "for Benson . . . [apostolic succession] was understood as the sacramental expression of the real presence of Christ through the power of the Holy Spirit in the whole life of his body the Church, the same Church now as it was in the beginning."[10] If Benson was critical of Roman and Anglo-Catholic trust in apostolic succession without a living and participating Christ, he took an equally dim view of the drift from a healthy trinitarianism that is revealed by the Bible and early church fathers. By no means anti-intellectual, Benson nonetheless maintained

9. Smith, *Benson*, 19–20.
10. Ibid., 22–23.

that scholasticism, and especially men such as Thomas Aquinas and Anselm, with their more extreme rationalism and its concomitant stress on man's knowledge of God through assent to propositions, unintentionally harmed the church. Benson regarded the scholastic method of rationalism as a major factor in the rise of modern agnosticism and atheism.[11]

In brief, Father Richard Benson believed that God created people with a capacity to know him in deeper ways than "mere intellectual apprehension." According to Benson, we are made to know God with "an active, experiential knowledge," by "participation in the divine life through union with Him." In a commentary on John 14:20 he wrote:

> The knowledge which constitutes eternal life is not a projected knowledge as of an external thing, but an experimental knowledge. We do not merely know about the Divine Relationships. That is only the dead form of knowledge which the intellect is capable of receiving. In spiritual life we know these Relationships by substantial identification in the Spirit of love. . . . This day of illumination is an inherent participation of the Divine self-knowledge.[12]

Martin Smith, a contemporary missioner priest in the SSJE and a keen student of Benson's works, wrote that Benson and his followers neither deny nor suppress man's intellect. Rather it is a "fundamental capacity as made in the image of God to transcend the limitations of his nature." Benson, according to Smith, wrote: "Our knowledge of Divine Being is in proportion as we are taken out of our own intellect to live in that very substance of God wherein the Three Divine Persons live

11. Ibid., 29–30.
12. Ibid., 30–31.

forever One." Benson insisted that "our nature is capable of receiving certain floating impressions respecting the Being of God but we must rise out of that nature if we are to know God."[13]

Benson's dynamic concept of humanity's knowledge of God makes it understandable that he was so critical of Christian faith as mere assent to propositions. Truly knowing the divine mystery, according to Benson, is "not the mere knowledge of a completed statement, but the continuous apprehension of a continuous reality, a living receptivity corresponding with a living object of contemplation." True knowledge of God is never static. "Man is called to a life of eternal energy in union with God by His Word and that life of active union is a life of progressive experience. The beatific vision will not be a stationary contemplation of a fixed form. . . . Man is called to rejoice in God's truth as a continually progressive acquisition."[14]

Lewis, of course, imbibed this teaching and began to walk a life of increased union with a living God. Hints of this dynamic relationship come out in *Surprised by Joy*. It is particularly evident in his *Letters to Malcolm* regarding the Eucharist and worship in a liturgical church.

For nearly twelve years C. S. Lewis walked the short trek from his rooms at Magdalen College, Oxford, to the immediately adjacent village of Cowley, where the Cowley Fathers lived and ministered. The Marston Street Monastery (they preferred to call it the Mission House) at this time had eighteen to twenty monks residing there in community living. The facility included living quarters

13. Ibid., 31.
14. Ibid.

for the priests, a few spartan guest rooms, a chapel for worship services, curtained confessional booths, and some austere counseling rooms, furnished with a table and two chairs, where a regular visitor like C. S. Lewis would meet with his spiritual director. The Mission House offered regularly scheduled worship services, including the celebration of the Eucharist and morning and evening prayer. Although the monastery was not a parish church, its priests became spiritual directors to a wide range of seekers and faithful Anglicans from a rather extensive English geographic area. Most of the priests were also available at regularly scheduled times to hear confessions. Consequently, a continuous throng of penitents would slip in to confess with a priest of their choice during his regularly scheduled times of availability. The Mission House also boasted a meeting room, where invited speakers such as C. S. Lewis offered lectures on topics of practical theology for students and members of the Anglican religious community. The Mission House also maintained an excellent little library and study facility, where people who were interested in reading the books of Richard M. Benson and related works were always welcome.[15]

Unless one of them was out of town, Lewis met with Walter Adams nearly every week. From this humble and relatively unknown monk, the increasingly famous Oxford don who hungered to grow in holiness learned to follow several essential paths to an increasingly Christ-like life. Adams stressed Lewis's need for daily prayer, weekly Communion, and the reading of the daily office

15. My sources on the Mission House and the ministry there during the years Lewis visited Father Adams come from several sources: a personal interview, July 19, 1988, with Fr. Martin Smith SSJE; a detailed letter from Fr. Alan Bean, who knew Fr. Adams and served with him; and ch. 5, "Cowley Fathers—A Monastic Experience," in David Bleakley, *C. S. Lewis at Home in Ireland* (Bangor, No. Ireland: Strandtown Press, 1998).

from the Anglican Book of Common Prayer. Lewis, like the Cowley Fathers, used the 1662 Prayer Book. Adams also advised Lewis to go to confession weekly, and to make an annual retreat of two to three days. Furthermore, Adams would have passed on to Lewis the SSJE's love for Holy Scripture, evangelism, passion for holiness, appreciation of the writings of the early church fathers, and a desire for "really" meeting the Lord Jesus Christ in the Eucharist and in prayer.

That Lewis heard Adams and embraced the tradition of the Anglican Reformers in the context of sacramental life and experimental living is evident from things he wrote in *Letters to Malcolm*: "The prayer preceding all prayers is, "May it be the real I who speaks. May it be the real Thou that I speak to.'" And in the Eucharist: "Here a hand from the hidden country touches not only my soul but my body."[16]

Adams also taught his able pupil to love the liturgy. Lewis described the liturgy as "one of the few very remaining elements of unity in our hideously divided church."[17] Furthermore, Lewis became convinced that a fixed form of service "is an advantage because the worshiper knows 'what is coming.'" One correspondent apparently wrote and questioned the use of written prayers. Lewis responded that "*ex tempore* public prayer has this difficulty; we don't know whether we can mentally join in until we've heard it—it might be phoney or heretical. We are therefore called upon to carry on a critical and a devotional activity at the same moment: two things hardly compatible." We are actually set free, not put in shackles, with a fixed or, as his inquirer put it, "rigid form."[18]

16. CSL, *Letters to Malcolm*, 109, 133.
17. Ibid., 15.
18. CSL to "A Lady," April 1, 1952, in WHL, *Letters*, 239–40.

In *Letters to Malcolm* he addressed the issue of liturgical services being too "conservative." There is "a good reason for their conservatism. Novelty simply as such, can have only an entertainment value." People don't or shouldn't go to church to be entertained. "They go to use the service, or, if you prefer, to enact it. Every service is a structure of acts and words through which we receive a sacrament, or repent, or supplicate, or adore." He wrapped up his point by arguing that the liturgy enables worshipers to do these things "best—when, through long familiarity, we don't have to think about it." Always the good teacher, capable of putting his points into word pictures that are easily understood, he wrote:

> As long as you notice, and have to count, the steps, you are not yet dancing but only learning to dance. A good shoe is a shoe you don't notice. Good reading becomes possible when you need not consciously think about eyes, or light, or print, or spelling. The perfect church service would be one we were almost unaware of; our attention would have been on God.[19]

In a letter he explained: "I don't see how the *ex tempore* method can help becoming provincial, and I think it has a great tendency to direct attention to the minister rather than to God." To Lewis, and certainly to his mentor Adams, if that happens, the whole purpose of worship is diverted if not lost. To Lewis, the liturgy was alive and he even told one friend that continuously repeating "*Sursum corda*" (lift up your hearts) had helped him overcome depression.[20]

19. CSL, *Letters to Malcolm*, 12.
20. CSL to "A Lady," April 1, 1952, in WHL, *Letters*, 239–40; Moynihan, *Letters*, numbers 8, 17, 33; and CSL to Griffiths, August 1962, in WHL, *Letters*, 305.

The Book of Common Prayer as well as liturgy gradually became an integral part of the fabric of C. S. Lewis's worship. Adams taught him to read the Psalter, praying through all 150 Psalms each month. Besides that, he taught Lewis to read the daily office and pray the appropriate collects as part of his devotions. That Lewis did this can be seen in many letters and publications. In a sermon delivered in Cambridge in 1954, he said, "Not long ago when I was using the collect for the fourth Sunday after Trinity in my private prayers . . ."[21] And in a pamphlet titled "Miserable Offenders: An Interpretation of Prayer Book Language" he noted that every day in Lent he and many faithful Anglicans say a prayer from the book asking God to give them "contrite hearts"—an attitude most befitting the Lenten season.[22]

Lewis not only quoted collects, but frequently quoted Psalms in letters, articles, and books, revealing how much his monthly attention to the whole Psalter filled his mind. Particular Psalms became important to his prayer and devotional life as they related to the church calendar, such as Psalm 45 on Christmas Day and Psalm 78 for Ascension. From Father Adams he learned to faithfully use the Psalter and use it in conjunction with the church calendar. The calendar, like the Psalms, impressed Lewis with centrality of Christ in all things. Of the calendar he wrote: "The complexity—the close texture—of all the great events in the Christian year impresses me more and more. Each is a window opening on the total mystery."[23] Thanks to these disciplines and insights gained from

21. "A Slip of the Tongue," in *Screwtape Proposes a Toast and Other Pieces* (London: Collins, 1965), 120.

22. Pamphlet published in Boston by The Advent Papers, n.d.

23. See *Reflections on the Psalms*. Chapter 12 is especially revealing. See also Moynihan, *Letters*, which is replete with references to liturgy, church calendar, and related Scripture; and CSL to "An American Lady," April 15, 1956, in Kilby, *Letters*, 52.

Adams, Lewis increasingly knew Christ as a "real" Lord and Savior who is ever present and inextricably central to life past, present, and future.

There is no question that Father Walter Adams and the monks in SSJE were very "high" churchmen. And it is obvious that Mr. Lewis increasingly found himself spending more time in the Anglo-Catholic room of the church. This is evident in his love for the church calendar and in his use of it as a way to identify with Christ through the year. Also Lewis embraced such Catholic traditions as the Veneration of the Cross in Good Friday services. His friend the author Harry Blamires told me that he was talking to Lewis on one occasion, telling him he was increasingly finding it necessary to worship with the Anglo-Catholics because they were "the only evangelicals left in the church." Lewis responded that there were still evangelicals in lower churches, intimating that he personally could be counted among them. Nevertheless, when Blamires said worshiping with the Anglo-Catholics could be difficult at times because of some of their practices, Lewis quickly came down on the other side: "Well, what for instance?" Blamires said he loved the Good Friday liturgy overall but found the part where they "were expected to walk up and kneel and kiss the foot of the crucifix" to be going too far, finally saying, "I couldn't do that." Immediately Lewis responded: "But you should. The body should do its homage." Blamires concluded that Lewis was at times quite high on the Anglican spectrum and at other times rather low. It all depended upon the doctrine and the practice.[24]

24. Lyle Dorsett, interview with Blamires, October 23, 1983, Wade Center.

Blamires understood how difficult it was to put Lewis in a precise location among the Anglican rooms. On the sacraments, for instance, he sided with the Anglo-Catholics, seeing marriage as a sacrament. Indeed, here was part of Lewis's problem with his bishop regarding the marriage to Joy Davidman Gresham. The official Anglican position, set forth in the Articles of Religion, expressly practices only two sacraments. Consequently, civil marriages are valid and must be honored, even if there has never been a marriage in the church. But C. S. Lewis could not see himself truly married to Joy after their civil ceremony. Only the "sacramental" marriage, performed by Father Peter Bide, freed them to live together as husband and wife.[25]

Lewis took an Adams-like Anglo-Catholic view of more than veneration of the cross and marriage; he embraced a doctrine of Purgatory as well. In *Letters to Malcolm* he wrote, "I believe in Purgatory." He acknowledged that "the Reformers had good reasons for throwing doubt on 'the Romish doctrine concerning Purgatory' as that Romish doctrine had then become." Years after Dante's *Purgatorio*, and especially by the sixteenth century with Thomas More's *Supplication of Souls*, Purgatory is perverted from a place for cleansing to "simply a temporary hell." Retribution replaces purgation. Rightly, the Reformers took this on. "The right view returns magnificently in Newman's Dream." There Lewis celebrates the image where the saved soul, at the very foot of the throne, begs to be taken away and cleansed. It cannot bear for a moment longer "with its

25. See Dorsett, *And God Came In*; George Sayer, *Jack*; and Walter Hooper, *C. S. Lewis: A Companion and Guide* (San Francisco: Harper, 1996), 633–34.

darkness to affront that light." "Religion," Lewis almost shouts, "has reclaimed Purgatory."[26]

If C. S. Lewis could embrace doctrines and practices like these, plus weekly confession to a priest—even a priest who listened and pronounced Christ's forgiveness not his own—there nevertheless were places this sometime Anglo-Catholic layman and writer would not go. As contrite as Lewis became, and as much as he humbled himself at the feet of this good and godly mentor, there were places where he absolutely drew the line. Lewis wrote to one friend that early on in his weekly meetings with Father Adams he found that "he is much too close to Rome. I had to tell him that I couldn't follow him in certain directions, and since then he has not pressed me."[27] Lewis never identified the disciplines he was urged to undertake, but it is likely they had to do with Mary, the mother of Jesus. One of Walter Adams's fellow monks informed me that Adams was famous, or infamous, inside the SSJE for being enthralled with Mary. "Don't be afraid of her," he exhorted people on retreats. And he frequently talked of "Her marvelous Annunciation, her Purification, her Immaculate Conception, her Glorious Assumption," frequently accompanied by a crescendo of "Lo, Mary." If Lewis encountered these words of veneration (and it is likely he did), he most certainly became distressed—and he was not alone. Some of the other priests who lived at the Mother House, including one outspoken man in particular, were "in a high state of protest," over these "Romish" outcries.[28]

<hr>

26. CSL, *Letters to Malcolm*, 139–40. See also CSL to Sister Penelope, September 17, 1963: "look me up in Purgatory," in WHL, *Letters*, 307.

27. CSL to Mary Neylan, April 30, 1941.

28. A letter in the possession of the author written by Father Alan Bean to Father Martin Smith, May 29, 1988, in answer to my questions about W. Adams and C. S. Lewis.

If Father Adams had urged Lewis to say "Hail Marys" or pray the rosary, there is no way the Oxford don would have obeyed. His position is clear in a letter written in answer to a question about incense and Hail Marys. "Incense," he said, "is merely a question of ritual; some find it helpful and others don't, and each must put up with its absence or presence in the church they are attending with cheerful and charitable humility." But Hail Marys were another matter to Lewis. This raises a doctrinal question. He questioned if "any creature, however holy," should be addressed with devotions. Saluting "any saint (or angel) cannot in itself be wrong any more than taking off one's hat to a friend." But the danger comes when "such practices start one on the road to a state (sometimes found in the R.[oman] C.[atholics]) where the B.[lessed] V.[irgin] M.[ary] is treated really as a divinity and even becomes the centre of the religion." He went on to say that "if the Blessed Virgin is as good as the best mothers I have known, she does not want any of the attention which might have gone to her Son diverted to herself."[29]

George Sayer, a Roman Catholic himself and a close friend of Lewis, informed me of a conversation he was privy to that took place between Lewis and Dr. Robert E. "Humphrey" Havard, a Roman Catholic and Jack's personal physician. Havard began to urge—and it was not the first time—Lewis to become a Roman Catholic. "But Jack said no. 'The important thing is to be a member of the Christian Church and which one is not so important.' But Havard would not relent, pushing on Jack a bit more." Lewis responded with some irritation that he was not tempted to share Havard's "heresies." When the doctor asked "what heresies," Jack said "Your

29. CSL to "A Lady," undated in WHL, *Letters*, 243.

views on the Virgin Mary and the doctrine of Papal Infallibility." And that ended the discussion.[30]

Alan Bede Griffiths, who like Sayer was one of Lewis's formal pupils who became a life-long friend, sometimes tried to nudge his old tutor toward the Roman Catholic Church. But he met the same stubborn resistance that Havard and others met. In one letter, Lewis summarized some of their differences as he saw them:

> One of the most important differences between us is our estimate of the importance of the differences. . . . You think my specifically Protestant beliefs a tissue of damnable errors; I think your specifically Catholic beliefs a mass of comparatively harmless human traditions that may be fatal to certain souls, but which I think suitable for you. Therefore I feel no duty to attack you. . . .[31]

It is obvious that C. S. Lewis could markedly disagree with Adams and still hold great love for him. Father Adams died on March 3, 1952, at age eighty-two. Adams's death staggered Lewis. He wrote to his Italian confidant, Father John Calabria, these words: "Pray for me, especially at present when I feel much an orphan because my aged confessor and most loving father in Christ has just died." Lewis went on to say that "while he was celebrating at the altar, suddenly, after a most sharp but (thanks be to God) very brief attack of pain, he expired; and his last words were, "I come, Lord Jesus."[32]

30. George Sayer to Lyle Dorsett in a personal conversation in July 1988.
31. CSL to Griffiths, quoted by Griffiths in James T. Como, ed., *C. S. Lewis at the Breakfast Table and Other Reminiscences* (London: Collins, 1980), 18.
32. CSL to Don Giovanni Calabria, April 14, 1952, in Moynihan, *Letters*, 71–72.

"I come, Lord Jesus" might have been Father Adams's last words, but he did not die celebrating the Eucharist at the altar. Where Lewis got this description of Adams's moment of death is unclear, but Lewis's promulgation of this event is erroneous. It is the kind of story that befits Adams's end, especially given Lewis's high regard for him. In fact, Lewis once said of Adams: "If I ever met a holy man, he is one."[33] But in truth Adams died not at church but at the home of a family that nursed him in his last days after the recurrence of a disease he contracted many years earlier as a missionary in India. According to the superior of the SSJE, Lewis must have confused Adams's death with an earlier incident at the Mother House.[34]

In any case, Lewis had learned much from Father Walter Adams. "I owed him a great deal. Everything he ever said to me was so simple that you might have thought it childish, but was always what was needed," he told one friend.[35] These generalizations were perhaps slightly exaggerated in the wake of his spiritual director's death, but other evidence corroborates Lewis's point. George Sayer heard from Lewis that the disciplines of prayer and fasting freed him from some earlier obsessive sins, bringing genuine freedom from a particular spiritual bondage.[36] Owen Barfield recalled that "at a certain stage in his life [certainly during his time with Adams] he deliberately ceased to take any interest in himself except as a kind of spiritual alumnus taking his moral finals. . . . I suggest that what began as deliberate choice became at length (as he had no doubt always intended it should) an ingrained and effortless habit

33. CSL to Mary Neylan, April 30, 1941.
34. See Bleakley, *C. S. Lewis at Home in Ireland*, 72–74.
35. CSL to Dom Bede Griffiths, May 17, 1952, BL.
36. George Sayer to Dorsett, 1988.

of soul." This transformation, of course, was precisely what Adams wanted for Lewis as he helped him along the pathways to holiness. "Self-knowledge, for him," Barfield observed, "had come to mean recognition of his own weaknesses and shortcomings and nothing more." Lewis had come to know, in Barfield's words, that there was "so much else—more interesting!"[37] Precisely. This was the vision of the "really present" Lord Jesus Christ, whom Benson called his men, like Adams, to help those in their spiritual core to know, see, and love. No wonder C. S. Lewis—who was always careful with words—said this about his SSJE friend:

> To me he meant a great deal. Indeed in all the years in which he was both my spiritual director and close friend I have met *no one* from whom I have derived so much help and counsel, and whose companionship I have valued so highly [italics mine].[38]

Certainly, no one living after 1940 had a more profound influence on C. S. Lewis's spiritual development than Father Walter Adams. Nevertheless, the picture of major elements involved in Lewis's spiritual formation would be incomplete without mentioning Sister Penelope CSMV (Community of St. Mary the Virgin). After Adams, no person did more to help him appreciate and partly enter into the Catholic room of Anglicanism.

In August 1939, Mr. Lewis received a letter from Sister Penelope telling him how *Out of the Silent Planet* had

---

37. Owen Barfield, "Introduction" in *Light on C. S. Lewis*, ed. Jocelyn Gibb (New York: Harcourt, Brace, & World, 1966), xvi.
38. Quoted in ibid.

given her "a joy and delight quite impossible to put into words."[39] This letter served as the spark that ignited a friendship that lasted almost a quarter-century, ending only when Lewis died in November 1963. Over the years this friendship grew through the exchange of well over a hundred letters, with a few personal encounters, as well. Lewis made visits to give lectures to those in the novitiate and to the junior sisters at Sister Penelope's convent of the Community of St. Mary the Virgin, located at Wantage, just a few miles outside of Oxford.

Eight years older than Lewis, Sister Penelope was born Ruth Penelope Lawson in Clint, Worcestershire, on March 20, 1890. Blessed with an unusually keen mind, she had parents who encouraged her to attend school, read widely, and purposefully discipline her intellectual gifts. Love for the Anglican Church came easily for young Ruth, because her father served as the vicar of Clint. She attended Worcester High School, where, according to Walter Hooper, "she developed a devotion to the Blessed Virgin and a love of Greek and Latin."[40] The headmistress of her school, Alice Ottley, taught Ruth many things, but two stood out, and she mentioned them in her spiritual autobiography, *Meditation of a Caterpillar* (1962):

> The first thing was that it was my duty as a Christian to examine my conscience before Communion, and to confess to God specifically what I found amiss. . . . [The second thing Miss Ottley] taught me personally and unknown to herself, on the evening of 15 March 1904 [as she prepared us for her confirmation in the Anglican church]

39. Quoted in Walter Hooper, *C. S. Lewis, A Companion and Guide* (New York: HarperCollins, 1996), 719.

40. See the biographical sketch of Sister Penelope in ibid., 718–20. Unless otherwise noted, the biographical information in the following paragraphs come from this succinct portrait.

. . . I knew with overwhelming certainty that she was living in a world of most intense reality, to which I was, as yet, a total stranger. I was outside it utterly, but it existed.[41]

Few people in the wider Anglican community—or in Lewis's whole range of friends—combined the sheer intellectual brilliance, love for books, ideas, and writing on the one hand, and the profound love for the Lord Jesus Christ on the other, as Sister Penelope. No wonder, then, that these two intellectuals reveled in each other's company through the mail and occasional personal visits. Lewis clearly admired Sister Penelope, commenting in one letter, "What a pleasant change to get a letter which does not say the conventional things."[42] They recommended books to each other, compared notes on each other's books, and committed to praying for each other daily.[43] Although the relationship was clearly reciprocal in encouragement, counsel, and advice, Lewis relied upon this Anglican nun in particular ways that fostered his spiritual formation—first as a Christian and second as an Anglican.

Sister Penelope lived eighty-seven years, and she served sixty-five of them as an Anglican religious. In 1912 she entered St. Mary's Convent, taking on the name Sister Penelope. Her order, founded by the Reverend W. J. Butler in 1848, is among the oldest Anglican orders. After taking her vows of chastity and obedience, she was encouraged to study theology, which she did at Keble College, Oxford. Under the guidance of Keble's warden, B. J. Kidd, and the renowned medievalist R. W.

41. *Meditation of a Caterpillar* (London: Faith Press, 1962), by a Religious of C. S. M. V., 24–28.

42. CSL to Sister Penelope, September 17, 1963, in WHL, *Letters*, 307.

43. CSL to Sister Penelope, November 6, 1957; October 9, 1941; August 9, 1939; December 22, 1942; and August 10, 1943, in Hooper, *Letters*, 470–71; 360; 321–23; 369–70; 372.

Hunt, she became well read in early church history, theology, and literature. The investment in her education proved to be wise. Sister Penelope wrote over two dozen books of popular theology, including her apologia for the Church of England, *The Wood for the Trees: An Outline of Christianity* (1935). A teacher and spiritual guide for the junior sisters, she also found time to translate seventeen volumes of writings of the church fathers. She is perhaps best known for her translation of Athanasius's *The Incarnation of the Word of God* (1944), for which C. S. Lewis wrote the introduction. Her scholarly productivity did not fall off with age. Indeed, at eighty she sprightly embarked upon the ambitious enterprise of translating St. Hugh of Victor.[44]

Walter Hooper, perhaps the most famous of all the students of Lewis's life and writing, knew both Lewis and Sister Penelope. He wrote that Lewis "spoke of her as his 'elder sister' in the Faith." Hooper also credits her as the person who "more than anyone helped him to appreciate the Catholic side of Anglicanism."[45] While there is little evidence to show that her impact matched that of Father Adams, Hooper's point is certainly well taken. Lewis increasingly grew open to the teachings and presuppositions of the Anglo-Catholic tradition once he began drinking deeply at the Cowley Father's well. The Ulster-born Protestant's correspondence shows he discussed with Sister Penelope what he learned from Adams and several Anglican writers. Because of his deep respect for the mind and spirituality of this Anglican nun, Lewis received her encouragement as he gradually moved farther into the higher Anglican room off the hallway of "mere Christianity." And if "no one," to use Lewis's own words about Father Adams, had so much influence on

44. See Hooper, *Companion*, 718–20.
45. Ibid., 719.

his spiritual development, this takes nothing away from Sister Penelope. After all, Lewis met with Father Adams weekly from 1940 to 1952. On the other hand, Lewis and Sister Penelope corresponded for eleven years after that, and it is doubtful if there was anyone else whom Lewis would have respected more on the subject of Anglican spirituality. In any case, for the last decade of his life she continually encouraged her spiritual brother to stay the course that both she and Adams had nudged him to travel.

If the first object one looks at upon waking in the morning is likely to have an impact on one's daily activities, it is important to know that Sister Penelope sent C. S. Lewis a photograph of the Shroud of Turin in the autumn of 1941. Lewis thanked her "for the photo of the Shroud." "It raises," he wrote, "a whole question on which I shall have to straighten my thoughts one of these days." A month later he wrote to Sister: "It has grown upon me wonderfully. . . . The great value is to make one realize that He really was a man, and once even a dead man. There is so much difference between a doctrine and a realization." Hooper maintains that Lewis "kept the photograph on the wall of the his bedroom for the rest of his life."[46]

Knowing Christ and experiencing the "realization of who He is" gradually became Lewis's life work. An essential part of his vocation, to Lewis's angle of vision, involved radical obedience to the One he desired to know. As Lewis discovered, uncompromised obedience is seldom easy, and it often involves forms of service that one, if free to choose, would never pick. For him, it necessitated answering thousands of letters, among them hundreds that required him to offer pastoral advice to countless people who had read his books and turned to him as their teacher and guide.

46. Ibid., 719–720.

6

RELUCTANT GUIDE

"I Wanted Them to Follow Christ"

One of C. S. Lewis's closest friends was Dr. Austin Farrer. Chaplain of Trinity College, Oxford, for almost twenty-five years, beginning in 1935, he became dean of Oxford's Magdalen College three years before Lewis died. Born in 1904 in London, Farrer became a priest of the Church of England in 1929. While preaching sermons and lecturing on theology, psychology, and literature, he wrote numerous books of such piercing insight that he was considered by many thoughtful observers to be one of the most interesting minds of the twentieth century. Lewis certainly agreed. In fact, he labeled Farrer "one of the most learned theologians alive," yet one who distilled his brilliance and learning so subtly and skillfully that even "the simple reader" can follow his thoughts.[1]

Neither Farrer nor Lewis were flatterers. What they wrote about each other carried the weight of honest assessment. Both of Farrer's brief portraits of Lewis, written after his friend died in 1963, constitute some of the most insightful work done on the celebrated Oxford writer. Two years after Lewis died Farrer wrote that "Lewis was an apologist from temper, from conviction, and from modesty. From temper, for he loved an argument. From conviction, being traditionally orthodox. From modesty because he laid no claim either to the learning which would have made him a theologian or the grace which would have made him a spiritual guide."[2]

Lewis would have agreed. He recognized his own temperamental and intellectual giftedness in apologetics, and he willingly and eagerly used these as God gave him opportunity. Beyond this he openly admitted that he had neither the call nor the formal training to be a theologian or pastor. Certainly he would have offered a resounding "amen" to the brilliant Farrer's assessment that he lacked the grace to be a spiritual guide.

But even geniuses can be wrong. The perspective of time and the preservation of primary sources reveal quite clearly that C. S. Lewis in fact became—and still is—a spiritual guide of such high caliber that it rivals his stature as a Christian apologist. How can this be for a man who had neither training nor ambition to be a spiritual director, and who never posted such a shingle on his door? Lewis himself unveiled the secret, albeit

---

1. See C. S. Lewis's "Preface" to Farrer's *A Faith of Our Own* (Cleveland: Word, 1961).

2. "The Christian Apologist," in Gibb, *Light on C. S. Lewis*, 24. See also, "In His Image," in Como, *C. S. Lewis at the Breakfast Table*, 242–44.

unknowingly, in a letter he wrote in 1950: "obedience is the key to all doors."[3]

Lewis's old spiritual director, Walter Adams, seldom missed an opportunity to remind people to "look after the roots and the fruits will look after themselves."[4] Being one of Adam's ablest and most dutiful pupils, Lewis took this exhortation to heart. He devoted part of each day to prayer, reading Scripture, and some form of worship. But to Professor Lewis, looking after roots required more than commonly prescribed disciplines. Deep watering of the roots, both Adams and Lewis agreed, required radical obedience to everything that the Lord Jesus required, regardless how small or mundane it seemed.

Obedience became extremely important to Lewis. He fully understood that Christians are "saved by grace through faith, and not of works," as the apostle Paul maintained. Nevertheless, Lewis cautioned that "whatever St. Paul may have meant, we must not reject the parable of the sheep and goats (Matt. XXV. 30–46)." He wrote that "no-one can make these two views consistent." To him it was a mystery, but in any case, "every man can be quite sure that every kind act he does will be accepted by Christ."[5] Love was all part of this fabric. In *Mere Christianity* he wrote, "I cannot learn to love my neighbour as myself until I learn to love God: and I cannot learn to love God except by learning to obey Him."[6] As he responded to one inquirer's question about

3. CSL to "A Lady," December 7, 1950, in WHL, *Letters*, 224–25.
4. Reminiscences of Adams from Alan Bean, given to me in a letter dated May 29, 1988, in author's private collection.
5. CSL to Mrs. Emily McLay, August 3, 1953, in WHL, *Letters*, 251–52.
6. CSL, *Mere Christianity*, 68.

developing a strong relationship with God, when Christ gives us an order, "it must be obeyed."[7]

It was radical obedience to a burdensome chore, what he once called "the bane of my life,"[8] that became the key to opening up Lewis's ministry as a spiritual guide. Precisely how the call came is unclear, but sometime in the late 1930s C. S. Lewis knew without doubt that God had appointed him to answer all of his mail. Friends such as Owen Barfield and George Sayer recalled that he sensed an inviolable obligation to answer fan letters. If a reader took the trouble to post a question or simply pen a letter of thanks for a book or talk that instructed the mind or "illumined the heart," Lewis promptly responded. Once *The Problem of Pain* came out in 1940, the letters to Lewis's house, The Kilns, appeared with greater frequency. And then when the "Screwtape Letters" were serialized in *The Guardian* for seven months (May–November) in 1941, followed up in book form in early 1942 and early 1943 in Britain and the United States respectively, Lewis became rather well known as a writer of Christian subjects. His BBC radio broadcast talks became immediately famous in 1941 and 1942, and they were hurried into print as *Broadcast Talks* (1942), *The Case for Christianity* (1943), *Christian Behaviour* (1943), and *Beyond Personality* (1944).

At the very time British and Americans increasingly went on the military offensive and took the torrents of war to Nazi Germany and imperial Japan in the early and mid-1940s, Mr. Lewis poured out his ammunition against the evil empire with an onslaught of books, articles, and sermons for those who sought freedom from

7. CSL to "A Lady," December 7, 1950, in WHL, *Letters*, 224–25. See also Arthur Mastrolia, *C. S. Lewis and the Blessed Virgin Mary: Uncovering a "Marian Attitude"* (Lima, Ohio: Fairway Press, 2000). He argues persuasively that obedience is a major theme in Lewis's writing.

8. CSL to Mrs. Ward, November 24, 1961.

the bondage of Satan. Besides *The Screwtape Letters* and the three little books that eventually became *Mere Christianity*, Lewis pelted the enemy with *Perelandra* (1943), *That Hideous Strength* (1945), and *The Great Divorce* (1946). Punctuating these book-length works were short pieces such as "Miracles" in *The Guardian* (1942), as well as "God in Three Persons" and "The Whole Purpose of the Christian," to name only two that appeared in several issues of *The Listener* in 1944.

Lewis's barrage of publications produced several immediate effects. First, he became relatively famous. Second, his income increased from escalating royalties and honoraria. And third, stacks of fan mail—growing to dozens and sometimes scores of letters each week—changed the order and rhythm of his life, because he quickly needed to commit several hours per week—and sometimes daily—just to follow God's call to answer the mail. He wrote to his friend Arthur Greeves in December 1941, noting that "in the aftermath of those Broadcast Talks I had an enormous pile of letters from strangers to answer." Some are "funny . . . but many [are] from serious inquirers who it was a duty to answer fully." Consequently, life was a bit different, and "letter writing . . . loomed pretty large."[9]

These changes in fame, income, and correspondence forced Lewis to be vigilant and keep short accounts with God lest he stumble and fall. Obedience required staying humble in the face of growing fame, but circumstances helped protect Lewis from too much pride. Like most writers, he received his share of unfavorable book reviews. Furthermore, he felt the sting of jealous

---

9. Lewis's friends told me about the mail, and he made frequent reference to it in letters: e.g., CSL to Greeves, December 23, 1941, in Hooper, *They Stand Together*, 491–93; CSL to Mr. McClain, March 7, 1945; CSL to Mrs. Ward, November 24, 1961; and see Sayer, *Jack*, 168, 169, 201, 218, 243.

colleagues who continually berated his evangelistic endeavors. Some went so far as to block his election to more than one Oxford University professorship for which he was nominated.

For example, Sheldon Vanauken claimed to have overheard some Oxford professors say that they were casting their votes against Lewis without even mentioning the name for whom they were voting. This is a credible story, because Oxford professor Helen Gardner, in her obituary of Lewis, revealed that "a suspicion had arisen that Lewis was so committed to what he himself called 'hot-gospelling'" that he would be ineffective as a professor. She wrote that "in addition, a good many people thought that shoemakers should stick to their lasts and disliked the thought of a professor of English Literature winning fame as an amateur theologian."[10]

Receiving ridicule for writing and teaching on Christian topics from his decidedly biblical, conservative position was nothing new for Lewis. He learned it was part of the price he must pay for faithfulness to his calling. The price became quite heavy, however, in Oxford University circles. Indeed C. S. Lewis remained "Mr. Lewis"—fellow and tutor at Magdalen College until 1954, when Magdalene College, Cambridge University, bestowed the honor of a professorship in Medieval and Renaissance English, a position he held until declining health forced his resignation in August 1963.

If Professor Lewis had plenty of help staying humble, he did have to take deliberate steps to obey the teachings of Jesus on money. A careful student of the Bible, Lewis knew that "it is more blessed to give than to receive" and he also understood the Master's warnings about the "deceit of riches" and that it was almost impossible

10. One of the best-documented descriptions of this professorship issue is in Hooper, *Companion*, 65–69.

for a rich man to enter the kingdom of heaven. To the point, George Sayer told me that Lewis commented that "money is not neutral." Understanding the danger of keeping money, leaning on it, or being caught up in materialism, he gave away most of his royalties—first in scattered and perhaps careless ways, but eventually more constructively through the creation of a charitable trust, The Agape Fund, overseen by his close friend and lawyer, Owen Barfield. These moneys went to feed, clothe, house, and pay medical and dental expenses for various people in need on both sides of the Atlantic. Likewise, several young people—David and Douglas Gresham, for instance, who were to become his stepsons—had their educations paid by the trust, as did at least one middle-aged man who needed help when he went back to college to study for ordination to the Anglican priesthood.[11]

The disciplines of turning the other cheek when criticized and marginalized, or holding possessions with an open hand, were never easy for C. S. Lewis, but he found them easier to practice than answering the deluge of mail that flooded upon him after 1939.

No one should assume that Lewis's obedience in writing so many carefully and thoughtfully crafted letters was well-intentioned but misguided legalism. To be sure he felt constrained to practice what he preached: "Thy will be done," he wrote in *Letters to Malcolm*; in "Membership" he insisted "obedience is the road to freedom"; and to one correspondent he stressed that "the

---

11. Sayer, *Jack*, 252. See also the preface to Clyde Kilby, ed., *Letters to an American Lady*; Dorsett, *And God Came In*, and interviews with Sayer and Barfield. See also Hooper, *Companion*, 623, 747.

beginning of sanctity" is "giving, not receiving."[12] But the fruit reveals the nature of the plant, and it is clear that Lewis's letter writing produced a bounteous harvest. Out of his seeds of obedience grew hundreds—eventually thousands—of letters replete with spiritual guidance to a wide range of inquirers, among them spiritual seekers, recent converts anxious about their next steps in the faith, people in bondage to sin, others struggling with temptations and guilt, and many healthy Christians simply in search of sound teaching that they apparently could not find elsewhere. Most of the individuals who received Lewis's personal correspondence were no doubt blessed. If they had not been, they probably would have discarded these thousands of letters that have been saved for posterity.

Indeed, one woman who must remain anonymous told me that she could not have survived the pain in her life without continually reading and rereading his pastoral letters written over several years. Lewis, of course, assumed his letters would be somewhat efficacious, and that is why he wrote with such personalized care. But for Lewis, writing the letters embodied more. As Clyde Kilby insightfully observed, for Lewis "taking time out to advise or encourage another Christian was . . . a humbling of one's talent before the Lord and also as much the work of the Holy Spirit as producing a book."[13] Lewis in fact answered one correspondent who feared she took up too much of his valuable time with, "You may put out of your head any idea of 'not having a claim' on any help I can give. Every human being, still more every Christian, has an absolute claim on me for any service I can render them without neglecting other

12. *Letters to Malcolm*, 39–40; CSL, "Membership," ch. 3, and the letter is to McCasland, August 2, 1954.
13. Preface to Kilby, *Letters*, 7.

116

duties."[14] This remarkable statement was hardly hollow rhetoric, considering that this extremely needy soul had been writing pain-filled letters to Lewis for a decade and would continue to do so for the next nineteen years.

Several of Lewis's friends and acquaintances told me that he confided to them his question of why God allowed him to be burdened by all of the mail. After all, that time could be used to write a book that might reach a wider audience. As Clyde Kilby, one of Lewis's acquaintances and an early student of Lewis's writing observed, "there seems no shred of idea [on Lewis's part] that these letters might eventually be published and thus take their place beside his other Christian works."[15] But as Lewis wrote to an English girl in 1949, the "important" part of spiritual life "is to keep on doing" what Jesus requires even when you don't understand why.[16]

Attempting to practice what he preached, Lewis answered the mail despite his inability to see God's wider purposes. Faithfulness in the mundane, offering up such a small thing as a few letters each day, afforded Lewis an opportunity to give over his meager loaves and fishes to Jesus Christ. But unlike the lad with the bits of food, Jack Lewis did not live to see the Lord multiply the gifts. Nevertheless, his small offering to each soul who wrote him was indeed multiplied into some of his most important books. With posthumous publication of many letters, especially *Letters to an American Lady*, *Letters to Children, Letters: C. S. Lewis / Don Giovanni*

14. CSL, Collection I, April 30, 1941, Wade Center. Note: Letters that are extremely personal are coded by a Collection number to protect the anonymity of the recipient. All letters are on file at the Wade Center. The precise citation will be revealed only at the discretion of the director or associate director of the Wade Center.

15. Clyde Kilby expressed this, as did George Sayer and several others with whom I spoke. See the Oral History Collection at the Wade Center for more evidence.

16. CSL to Sarah, April 3, 1949, in *Letters to Children,* 25–27.

Calabria, and the more eclectic collections edited by Warren H. Lewis and Walter Hooper, a growing reading public now has access to some of C. S. Lewis's most important teaching and spiritual counsel. For many of us, Lewis continues to be our teacher and spiritual guide.

The reluctant spiritual director became an unusually effective guide for several reasons. First, besides a deep sense of calling to answer mail, he treated each correspondent as if he or she were as important as the king or queen of England. In Lewis's eyes, of course, they all were indeed equal in importance. His letters manifest what he preached in "The Weight of Glory" in 1940: "There are no ordinary people, you have never talked to a mere mortal. Nations, cultures, arts, civilizations—these are mortal, and their life is to ours as the life of a gnat. But," he continued in this June 8, 1941 sermon at the Church of St. Mary the Virgin, Oxford, "it is immortals who we joke with, work with, marry, snub and exploit—immortal horrors or everlasting splendours." We should, therefore, do all we can to nudge people toward Christlikeness.[17]

Second, Lewis was always an encourager. He affirmed his correspondents' dignity and promised to pray for many of them on a daily basis. "I will certainly put you in my prayers" he wrote to one woman; he assured another with a family, "you are all in my prayers," and to a woman questioning if Christ is God: "you are always in my prayers." Definitely a man of his word, Lewis never promised prayers for the occasional correspondent. He

17. This message is reprinted in *The Weight of Glory*, ch. 1.

reserved this gift to those with whom he corresponded over extended periods.[18]

Austin Farrer underscored the fact that Lewis's "characteristic attitude to people in general was one of consideration and respect. He did his best for them, and he appreciated them." He further observed that "the impact of his writings sufficiently shows that he had a fundamental sympathy with the public for which he wrote, a sympathy based partly on the experience of teaching, partly on a scrupulous attention to the letters that readers, sane or mad, simple or sophisticated, wrote him from all over the world." And, Farrer concluded, "he answered them all."[19]

It is probable that Lewis confessed to Father Walter Adams his exasperation over all the mail, especially when so many of these epistles were rife with self-pity and massive self-absorption. It is hard to imagine that he could have avoided some ill feelings toward people who were cranks, ignoramuses, or seekers of approval for what was clearly sinful behavior. Adams, we know, was famous within Cowley circles for being able to "put up with ghastly people out of genuine compassion," of whom there were many who showed up for counsel.[20] No doubt Lewis received instruction for pastoring such people from his experienced director, and he employed what he learned with patience and grace.

Besides seeing his correspondents as important, encouraging them, and eliciting lessons from Father Adams on how to work with difficult people, Lewis be-

---

18. These are all direct quotations from letters in the Wade Center. Hundreds of these phrases appear, but only to those with whom Lewis carried on extended correspondence. See Letter Collections I, II, III, IV and *Latin Letters* and Kilby, *Letters to an American Lady*.

19. Farrer, "In His Image," in Como, *C. S. Lewis at the Breakfast Table*, 243.

20. Letter from Fr. Alan Bean, May 29, 1988, in author's collection.

came markedly effective because of his transparency about his own personal flaws. In short, he admitted he struggled with sin like everyone else. Therefore, he became human to people and this gave them hope. Many of his letters contain references to his own sinful behavior. "I know all about the despair of overcoming chronic temptations," he told one person who bewailed slipping into the same sin again. "It is not serious, provided self-offended petulance, annoyance at breaking records, impatience etc. don't get the upper hand. No amount of falls will really undo us if we keep on picking ourselves up each time." The great encourager who admitted his flaws offered sound biblical advice. Remember "we shall of course be v.[ery] muddy and tattered children by the time we reach home. But the bathrooms are all ready, the towels put out, and the clean clothes in the airing cupboard. The only fatal thing is to lose one's temper and give it up. It is when we notice the dirt that God is most present in us; it is the v.[ery] sign of His presence."[21] Similarly, Lewis confessed his habit of grumbling,[22] and to a woman in New Zealand he admitted, "Oh how you touch my conscience! I treated my own father abominably and no sin in my whole life now seems to be so serious." He went on to mention his astonishment at the care (or even the affection) with which he had "been able to treat in other men the very same characteristic [he] was so impatient with in [his] father."[23]

Lewis's ability to treat each letter writer with dignity, his unflagging skill at honest encouragement and affirmation even when it must have been difficult, plus his skill at identifying with his correspondents through admission of his own flaws, all conspired to make him an

21. CSL to "A Lady," Jan. 20, 1942, in WHL, *Letters*, 199.
22. CSL to Sister Penelope, October 9, 1941, in WHL, *Letters*, 194.
23. CSL to Miss Rhona M. Bodle, March 24, 1954, BL.

effective soul caregiver. Equally important, however, was his straight talk and tough love. There was no space in his letters for cheap grace. He insisted that discipleship is costly. Obedience is required. Forgiveness covers all who truly repent, and Bible truth needs to be confronted. All these positions Lewis conveyed in clear prose even at the risk of offending the inquirer.

Numerous themes emerge from a careful examination of the letters C. S. Lewis wrote after 1939, yet foremost in his thinking and writing was each person's need to see Jesus Christ, to know and love him. Indeed, Christocentricity is the major theme throughout his letters. To a woman in Baltimore, Maryland, who just never seemed to grow in her faith, he said, "I must say what I think is true. Surely the main purpose of our life is to reach the point at which 'one's own life as a person' is at an end. One must in this sense 'die,' become 'naught,' relinquish one's freedom and independence. 'Not I, but Christ that dwelleth in me'—'He must grow greater and I must grow less'—'He that loseth his life shall find it.'"[24]

A well-meaning person, thinking she was encouraging him by reporting that her friends were reading his works and attempting to emulate him, elicited this response: "I am shocked to hear that your friends think of following me. I wanted them to follow Christ. But they'll get over this confusion soon, I think."[25] In the same spirit of encouraging people to stay focused on the Lord Jesus Christ, he exhorted a little girl through a tender letter written less than a month before he died: "If you con-

24. CSL to Mary, March 28, 1961, in Kilby, *Letters*, 95.
25. CSL to a woman, August 2, 1954, Letters Collection IV.

tinue to love Jesus, nothing much can go wrong with you, and I hope you may always do so."[26]

For Lewis, knowing Christ and being "in Him" offered the only path to peace, holiness, and eternal life. He also believed, beyond a shadow of doubt, that everyone must receive help from the body of Christ to enter this sanctification process. "The Church is Christ's body," Lewis insisted, and this is the body "He works through." You need "to get inside" if you are to grow and reach non-believers. Because of your faith in Him, "you are giving Him, as it were, a new finger," when you get yourself into the church.[27] The church has theologians to help guide us, and finally it must be understood that "the Church is the Bride of Christ" and that "we are members of one another."[28]

New believers who sought direction were pointed to spiritual disciplines. Sometimes he set forth a bare-bones list of practices. "Congratulations . . . on your . . . decision." Now as what to do next, he said to one of these, "I suppose the normal next step, after self-examination, repentance and restitution, is to make your Communion; and then to continue as well as you can, praying as well as you can . . . and fulfilling your daily duties as well as you can." He went on to say that if she decided she could be helped by a confessor, she should be sure to hear from him that she is absolved. Likewise he promised to help her find a good director if she needed assistance.[29]

26. CSL to Ruth, October 26, 1963, in CSL, *Letters to Children*, 111.

27. CSL to "A Lady," December 8, 1941, in WHL, *Letters*, 196.

28. CSL to "A Lady," November 28, 1950, in WHL, *Letters*, 223; CSL, "Membership."

29. CSL to "A Lady," January 4, 1941, in WHL, *Letters*, 191–92.

Usually he wrote rather explicit challenges on each of the disciplines, often stressing the necessity of beginning with fearless and searching moral inventory followed by genuine confession and repentance. When you feel guilty, he said, remember that the devil loves to impose a "cloud of unspecified guilt feeling . . . by which he lures into despair." Demand "details, please." Of course, if there is "a particular sin on your conscience, repent and confess it."[30] From personal experience he could challenge: If you suffer humiliation at the hands of unkind people, get your eyes off of self. "We would mind humiliation less if [we] were humbler."[31] And for one who was too introspective and despondent, he urged the biblical prescription to "rejoice, and always rejoice."[32]

Lewis never shied away from confronting people's often raised questions regarding sexual temptation and sin. He argued that marriage is important for many biblical reasons. It is ordained of God. And one of the reasons is "the biological aspect." Many people cannot consistently remain chaste as God requires. Therefore, one excellent alternative is marriage.[33] Lewis gave no ground to the person who saw masturbation as an option for how to cope with sexual temptation. After discarding all the humbug about the physical harm from autoeroticism, he got to the core of the matter: "For me the real evil of masturbation w[oul]d. be that it takes an appetite which, in lawful use, leads the individual out of himself to complete (and correct) his own personality in that of another (and finally in children and grandchildren) and turns it back; sends the man into the prison of himself, there to keep a harem of imaginary

30. CSL to Mary, July 21, 1958, in Kilby, *Letters*, 74–75.
31. CSL to Mary, March 31, 1954, in ibid., 28–29.
32. CSL to Don Giovanni, December 26, 1951, in Moynihan, *Letters*, 69–70.
33. CSL, April 18, 1940, Letters Collection I.

brides." Lewis went on to say that "this harem, once admitted, works against his ever getting out and really uniting with a real woman. For the harem is always accessible, always subservient, calls for no sacrifices or adjustments, and can be endowed with erotic and psychological attractions which no woman can rival." Finally, among these fantasies the man "is always adored, always the perfect lover; no demand is made on his unselfishness, no mortification ever imposed on his vanity. In the end, they become merely the medium through which he increasingly adores himself."[34] From Lewis's angle of vision, any sexual activity, including homosexuality, outside of monogamous heterosexual marriage is outside the will of God.[35]

Always fast to get beyond fixation on sin, Lewis accentuated the positive. After honest repentance there are particular disciplines that enrich the soul because they are effective channels of grace. Next to becoming part of a local church, one must be baptized and confirmed. Beyond these basic responsibilities, beginning a life vitalized by prayer stands at the top of Lewis's list of channels of grace. "I v.[ery] much doubt if I'm good enough at prayer myself to advise others." Nevertheless, he urged "first thing in the morning and the last thing at night are good times," although he didn't find that "they are the best times for one's main prayers." Drawing upon his own experience, "I prefer sometime in the early evening, before one has got sleepy—but of course it depends on how your day is mapped out." And do not be concerned if you do not feel like praying. "It is an act of the will (perhaps strongest when there is some disinclination to contend against) that God values, rather than a state of emotions." God receives

34. CSL to a man, March 6, 1956.
35. CSL to Vanauken, May 1954, in Vanauken, *A Severe Mercy*, 147.

our prayers as a gift, and then He sometimes gives us a gift of feelings. But these are often given "indirectly thro' the state of our body, health, etc, tho' there are direct kindlings from Him too." He acknowledged that it is sometimes difficult to keep properly focused on God "for more than a few seconds. Our minds are in ruins before we bring them to Him [and] the rebuilding is gradual." For this problem the ever-practical guide urged his correspondent "to practice concentration on other objects twice a week quite apart from one's prayers: i.e. (say, a flower) and try for few minutes to attend exclusively to it, quietly (never impatiently) rejecting the train of thought and imagination wh. keep starting up."[36]

The purpose of prayer is to get into God's presence, praising Him and allowing His Spirit to transform you into the likeness of his Son. Prayer is also important, he assured those who inquired, in helping you make decisions such as which church to attend or enabling one to overcome fear.[37]

Another theme that frequently appears in Lewis's letters of spiritual guidance is the importance of the Bible. His innumerable letters urge people to read for hope, strength, and guidance. He particularly advocated the New Testament, with strong emphasis on Christ's teachings in the Gospels.[38] Lewis knew people

---

36. CSL to Miss Rhona M. Bodle, January 3, 1948, BL.
37. See for example, CSL to "A Lady," March 18, 1952, in WHL, *Letters*, 239; CSL to "A Lady," July 17, 1953, in WHL, *Letters*, 250–51; and CSL to Mary, February 24, 1961, in Kilby, *Letters*, 93–94. See also ch. 2 of this book, on prayer.
38. See ch. 3 of this book, on Scripture.

needed Christ, and the only pure source to learn of his life and teachings is Scripture. But Lewis did more than point people to the texts that illumined their situations. When they had serious questions about the Bible, he took great pains to answer as specifically as he could. A common question regarded faith and works. To what extent are works related to salvation and discipleship? Always as candid as possible and admitting that some things are difficult to understand, he offered some clear teaching that at once helped the questioner but stayed faithful to the plenary meaning of Scripture. To one man he wrote, "Our Lord himself speaks as if all depends on faith, yet in the parable of the sheep and the goats all seems to depend on works. . . . The best I can do about these mysteries is to think that the N.T. gives us a sort of double vision: A. Into our salvation as eternal fact, as (and all else) is in the timeless vision of God. B. Into the same thing as a process worked out in time. Both must be true in some sense but it is beyond our capacity to envision both together."[39] In somewhat the same way he wrote to others on this honest question about salvation and its relation to faith and works. "We must not interpret any one part of Scripture so that it contradicts other parts," he told one correspondent. "We must not use an apostle's teaching to contradict that of our Lord. . . . Whatever St. Paul meant" about faith and predestination, "we must not reject the parable of the sheep and the goats." We would do well to humble ourselves before the Bible and admit that it contains mystery. Finally, if works don't secure our salvation, they must be the fruit of it.[40]

39. CSL to Mr. Stuart D. Robertson, May 6, 1962. This letter can be found in the Wade Center.
40. CSL to Mrs. Emily McLay, August 3, 1953, in WHL, *Letters*, 251–52.

Feeding the soul on confession, repentance, prayer, and the Bible were often lifted up by Lewis as staples for a healthy spiritual diet. But nourishment of the soul was incomplete, to his mind, if a person did not go to church and receive Holy Communion. He pointedly told a woman with a question about Holy Communion that the Lord requires it, and that He requires that we take it in fellowship with other believers. Lewis admitted that although his personal inclinations were to go to God in solitude, and indeed he admitted he spent much time in private prayer and reading, he nonetheless partook of regular worship that included the Eucharist in the church, because this is a biblical mandate.[41]

His letters to new believers are salted with exhortations to be purposeful in their worship by partaking of Holy Communion. The inference is that Communion once a quarter or even once a month is a form of spiritual fasting he would never recommend. He told Mrs. A. J. McCaslin, for example, to "be very regular in your prayer and communion," and he told someone else to "be sure your Communions are frequent and regular."[42] And he celebrated with those who prepared to receive the Eucharist for the first time. He offered hearty congratulations to a young woman before her first Communion, but warned her not to "count on any remarkable sensations, either at this on your first (or fifty-first) Communion."[43] And to a goddaughter, he sent exhortations not to "expect . . . count on . . . [or] demand . . . feelings" when you first receive Communion. "The things that are hap-

41. CSL to Mrs. Van Deusen, July 1, 1950; also to Mary, March 19, 1963, in Kilby, *Letters*, 111–12.

42. CSL to Mrs. A. J. McCaslin, August 2, 1954; CSL to Miss Gladding, June 7, 1945.

43. CSL to Miss Rhona M. Bodle, January 3, 1948, BL.

pening to you are quite real things whether you feel as you w[oul]d. wish or not." Communion feeds your soul like food feeds your body, regardless of taste or feeling. The important thing is to obey Jesus on this. Lewis's exhortations were almost identical to the words of that famous eighteenth-century Anglican John Wesley, who said we are commanded to commune whether we feel immediate benefit or not. "But undoubtedly we shall find benefit sooner or later, though perhaps insensibly. We shall be insensibly strengthened, made more fit for the service of God, and more constant in it."[44]

To C. S. Lewis's mind, reading books never rivaled prayer, worship, and participation in the body of Christ, Bible reading, or Holy Communion as soul nourishment. But he certainly placed reading books written by his favorite Christian authors high on his list of disciplines useful for spiritual healing, protection, and growth. Although he was much too astute to recommend the same books for each needy or hungry soul, he prescribed some authors with marked regularity. Lewis urged George MacDonald's three-volume *Unspoken Sermons* on many correspondents. In the early 1940s, despite the fact that this work was out of print, people could secure a set from secondhand book dealers. It is probable that Lewis's urging MacDonald on people created such scarcity that he felt constrained to edit *George MacDonald: An Anthology* in 1946. Once this little volume was in print in the United States and Great Britain, he frequently recommended it because,

44. CSL to Sarah, April 3, 1949, in CSL, *Letters to Children*, 25–27. And J. Ernest Rattenbury, *The Eucharistic Hymns of John and Charles Wesley* (London: Epworth Press, 1948), 172.

as he admitted, it had become almost impossible to find the unabridged set.[45]

Occasionally Lewis recommended other books by George MacDonald as tonics for the soul. He was especially keen on two novels, *Annals of a Quiet Neighborhood* and its sequel, *A Seaboard Parish*. He also pointed to two fairyland novels, *Lilith* and *Phantastes*, for those who he believed would appreciate them. While he acknowledged the awkwardness of MacDonald's prose, he admitted that the nineteenth-century Scotsman was his "mentor." Lewis, of course, never met MacDonald, because the author and sometime pastor died in 1905. Lack of personal interaction notwithstanding, Lewis confessed to never writing a book without borrowing something from that forgotten author of nearly fifty books.[46]

Several other authors frequently reappear in Lewis's most-prescribed list. G. K. Chesterton's *Everlasting Man* and *Orthodoxy* were urged on seekers after spiritual truth. Gustav Aulén's *Christus Victor* he recommended to people seriously grappling with the doctrine of salvation. For correspondents probing theological or ecclesiological issues, he sometimes pointed to works by Augustine, Richard Hooker, Jeremy Taylor, or John Henry Newman. People hungering for the deeper life were referred to Brother Lawrence, *The Practice of the Presence of God*, William Law, *A Serious Call to the Devout and Holy Life*, Thomas à Kempis, *The Imitation of Christ*, and books by Richard Meux Benson, Baron Friedrich Von Hugel, and Julianne of Norwich. And for people whose souls Lewis knew would be strengthened by poetry, his favorite was George Herbert.

45. See, for example, CSL to "A Lady," March 26, 1940, in WHL, *Letters*, 179–82; CSL to Mrs. Margaret Gray, May 9, 1961, in WHL, *Letters*, 298–99.
46. See Lewis's *George MacDonald: An Anthology* (London: Geoffrey Bles, 1946), preface.

Not all books Lewis recommended were offered in a context of spiritual care or direction. Always the teacher, Lewis received numerous letters from intellectually hungry people who sought his advice about a wide range of literary, historical, religious, and theological matters. Unusually eclectic in his own reading and study—yet never a dilettante—Lewis recommended what he knew, and the works ranged from pre-sixth-century church fathers down to his contemporaries such as Charles Williams, Austin Farrer, Dorothy L. Sayers, and his wife, Joy Davidman.[47] In brief, books had shaped much of his thinking. Therefore, he urged others to read his printed treasures.

47. Lewis's personal library, especially the books with endpaper and marginal notations, reveals important glimpses into his thinking. The library is housed at Wheaton College's Marion E. Wade Center. The Wade Center's collection of Lewis letters is filled with Lewis's recommendations of books.

7

STEERING THROUGH TROUBLED WATERS

"Keep Your Eye on the Helmsman"

Despite the massive numbers of letters that found their way to Lewis's house each day, he managed to answer them with care, even going so far as drawing illustrations of animals and people in some of the letters to children. This is all the more remarkable considering he faithfully executed his university duties, wrote books, gave sermons and lectures outside of the academic community, and tended to domestic responsibilities that increased over the years.

Besides all of these duties and responsibilities there is a strikingly impressive dimension to Lewis's soul care ministry that laid a great burden on this already heavily committed man. There was a group of people—mostly women—who sought soul care from Lewis that went far beyond what his typical correspondent required. These people comprised a motley congregation who lived as close as Oxford and as far away as New Zealand. Citizens of the United Kingdom, Italy, the United States of America, and far-flung British Commonwealth countries, these people had only two things in common: their souls needed objective and long-term care and they knew in their hearts that C. S. Lewis could help them. Lewis faithfully wrote to these souls, and some of them he even met in person for prayer and one-to-one counseling.

The evidence shows that the number of these needy people grew after the early 1940s. It is also apparent that Lewis first developed compassion and eventually a sense of duty so great that it caused him to devote much time for them in prayer. When he wrote as he did to one English woman, "read your New Testament . . . pray for guidance . . . obey your conscience in small as well as in great matters," he agonized in prayer over these issues with her, as he did for others in similarly distressful circumstances.[1] Increasingly common were such phrases as this one for an American: "You have been in my daily prayers ever since your first letter."[2]

Like any person overworked and wrapped in growing stress, Lewis sometimes felt despondent, oppressed, and resentful toward those very people God called him to love and serve. He took his problem to Father Adams in January 1942. Adams told him to "abbreviate" his prayers. Consequently Lewis began saying briefer daily prayers for some people but saving the longer prayers for two days a week. This practice eased the strain, he told one friend, and consequently the prayer ministry "ceases to be irksome and is often a delight."[3]

One of Mr. Lewis's former students at Oxford, Harry M. Blamires, remembered his mentor's relationship with

1. See CSL to "A Lady," June 13, 1951, in WHL, *Letters*, 232–33.
2. Letter Collection IV, September 19, 1954, BL.
3. Letter to Mrs. Neylan, January 20, 1942. This letter can be found in the Wade Center.

pupils in a way that captures his connections with people who became his "spiritual" students through mail and occasional meetings:

> He was personally interested in his pupils and permanently concerned about those who became his friends. Though he was a most courteous and considerate person his frankness could, when he wanted, cut through the ordinary fabric of reticence with a shock of sudden warmth or sudden devastation, indeed of both at once. No one knew better how to nourish a pupil with encouragement and how to press just criticism when it was needed, without causing resentment.[4]

This spirit of candid criticism couched in honest concern and encouragement typified a relationship reflected in one series of letters written over a period of three decades.

During the 1980s my wife Mary and I made at least one trip a year to the United Kingdom.[5] We conducted oral history interviews with people who knew C. S. Lewis, and we sought to collect Professor Lewis's correspondence for the Lewis collection at Wheaton College's Marion E. Wade Center. Although many of Lewis's letters have gone the way of most correspondence, we were able to do our small part in the noble effort of many people such as Clyde Kilby, Walter Hooper, and Marjorie Mead to rescue over 3,000 Lewis letters from mold, mil-

4. Blamires quoted by Warren H. Lewis, "Memoir," in WHL, *Letters*, 17.
5. The following account of how I discovered this collection of letters and learned of their profound impact is based on two interviews with the recipient I will call Mrs. Jones. Her name, as well as the names of others, and a few circumstances have been changed to keep the personal relationship between

dew, trash bins, and fires. Through one of our English contacts we learned of a widow who resided in a small village in southern England. We contacted Grace Jones, who acknowledged she corresponded with C. S. Lewis for thirty years. She invited us to her small cottage on a July afternoon in 1985.

Mrs. Jones cordially welcomed us, served tea, and listened to our plea for help in gathering and preserving Lewisiana for posterity. After a few moments of studied silence, she agreed that our enterprise was worthy and then got up and left the room. She returned carrying a stack of letters, including ones Mr. Lewis had written to her as well as a few handwritten drafts of letters she eventually typed and mailed to him. With the care one might use to handle an ancient family heirloom, the letters were handed over to me. She then urged us to glance through the collection and see if they were of any value to our collection. After we had perused a dozen or so letters, I assured Mrs. Jones that she possessed one of the most significant collections of Lewis's unpublished work that I had seen.

Mrs. Jones gathered the letters up, placed them on the tea table, and then proceeded to reveal the context of this correspondence that spanned a period from summer 1931 through late 1960. With tear-filled eyes she expressed an enormous debt to Mr. Lewis. She confessed that his spiritual counsel first kept her from committing suicide in 1932. His continued care further helped her move from the darkness and agony of unbelief to faith in Jesus Christ. Over the years

---

C. S. Lewis and this person in sacred anonymity. Her charity in telling her story and opening her correspondence was done for two reasons. First, she hoped Professor Lewis could be honored for his life-changing thirty-year-long counsel to her and, indirectly, to her family. Second, she hoped the counsel she received would help other confused and hurting souls who can never have the privilege of knowing Mr. Lewis.

Lewis helped her survive some difficult trials: first her marriage and then, as she described it, "the burden of raising children."

After pouring some of her story out to us, Mrs. Jones revealed that these letters had been an essential source of spiritual support over the years. Indeed, she confided how she frequently reread them when her faith wavered and she needed strength to keep on living. Besides these letters, she mentioned how her set of George MacDonald's *Unspoken Sermons*—purchased at the behest of Lewis—became a powerful source of inspiration. Her mentor wisely urged her to read these sermons as a useful guide for interpreting the most important themes of Scripture.

About two hours after our arrival, we thanked Mrs. Jones for trusting us enough to share some of her life story. As we stood to leave, she picked up her precious collection of letters, handed them to me, and said, "You can have these for the Wade Collection." Although the purpose of our visit carried hopes of getting an interview and her letters, I glanced at the handwritten epistles again and saw the fingered edges soiled from years of use by a thirsty soul. I looked at Mrs. Jones and said, "Thank you for this beautiful act of charity. But no, I can't take these. It would be like walking away with your beloved Bible or Book of Common Prayer. With your permission, however, may we borrow these treasures long enough to make copies?"

Grace Jones's face exploded with gratitude. I couldn't tell if she exuded surprise or relief that God had answered her prayer. Perhaps it was both. In any case the afternoon was too far gone to find a photocopy shop that evening. So we made copies the next day and placed the originals back in her hands the next afternoon.

The Jones-Lewis letters provide a rather clear picture of how Lewis cared for one needy soul.[6] Grace first wrote to Lewis in summer 1931, about the time he returned to the Christian faith. One of her professors at another college had recommended Lewis as a tutor to help Grace prepare for her final university examinations in literature. Lewis agreed to help and then outlined a course of reading, essays, and tutorials. After an extended season of preparation, she took her exams but failed to earn a degree. The effect was devastating. She was convinced she had a "Fourth Class Mind," but Lewis wrote, "You must not run away with the idea that you are a Fourth Class mind." He proceeded to point out "what really ruined" her was not her mental acumen but that her essays were "very short and general." He went on to say, "I blame myself for not extorting more essays from you . . . but I doubt if that was the whole cause." Finally, he assured her, "You have not done yourself justice. Your real quality is far beyond the work you did in school. This is cold comfort to you with the world to face!—but at least it is said quite sincerely and not merely for sake of consoling you."[7]

Grace found some hope in Lewis's candid letter. She held on to it, reread it often, and gradually picked herself up and moved forward. A half decade later she was teaching, married, and able to take Lewis up on his promise: "If there should at anytime be any way in which I can be of use to you, let me know at once." She was reading poetry with some gusto and sought out Lewis's advice for a bibliography of criticism.[8]

6. The letters will be cited as Collection I, and only the dates will be used.

7. I: July 28, 1932.

8. I: March 8, 1937.

136

After Grace married, Lewis usually inquired after her husband, in part because he had a genuine interest but certainly to keep the relationship above anything that even suggested a budding romantic interest. Consequently, Mr. Jones wrote to Lewis from time to time. In 1937 he invited his wife's old tutor to come to their community to do an evangelistic lecture. Lewis responded, "Your offer is attractive to the hot-gospeller in me, but after a lot of thought I feel I must refuse. I have no notion how to handle such an audience."[9]

Mr. Jones probably wanted Lewis to speak for his wife's benefit as much as for others' in town. Her exchanges with Mr. Lewis in the late 1930s and the early 1940s made it clear that she was a depressed soul who lacked the blessing of Christian faith. She admitted suffering from neuroses, discussed being treated by a psychologist and a psychoanalyst. She likewise confessed to being petrified that she would raise her children wrong during what these analysts told her are the most formative years of their lives. At Lewis's urging, she did read his *Pilgrim's Regress* and Chesterton's *Orthodoxy*. She also read the Gospels. But she bluntly admitted she found Lewis and Chesterton a bit "sentimental," whereas the "personality" described in the Gospels simply disappointed her.[10]

Over at least two years Lewis endured personal visits during which at least once her children were dreadfully unruly in the house. Indeed, Mrs. Jones apologized for their behavior, yet insisted that the more permissive approach to child rearing—some of which she gleaned from the bombastic agnostic Bertrand Russell—was right on target. She said children need to be taught to lead, not become slave-mindedly obedient. Lewis

9. I: May 5, 1937.
10. I: Jones to Lewis, Holy Week, 1940.

responded by maintaining a strikingly different angle of vision. "I think that there is in existence a Being so intrinsically authoritative that obedience is the essential business of a human being." He also said that "nearly everyone will find himself in the course of his life in positions where he ought to command and positions where he ought to obey. . . . You can't begin training a child to command until it has reason and age enough to obey: that is teaching it the end of obedience as such—without prejudices to the views it will later hold as to who should obey whom, or when, or how much."[11]

Lewis wrote nearly four pages trying to show Mrs. Jones that psychoanalysis might have its place, but he made it clear that he thought it offered no panacea for the human condition. He especially discounted one doctor's conclusion that her child is "nervous." Lewis said he "probably is right in the sense that she is not, and never will be, perfectly wise, good, and happy." To Lewis the problem with the doctor is that he equates "happiness" and "normality." And of course here is where Christianity enters the situation. Therefore, he urged her—in three more long pages—to read the Gospels again—this time not looking for the personality she wanted or expected to find. In fact, he said, "the first thing you find is that we are simply not invited to speak, to pass any moral judgment on Him, however favorable; it is only too clear that He is going to do whatever judging there is; it is we who are being judged, sometimes tenderly, sometimes with stunning severity. . . . The first real work of the Gospels on fresh readers is, and ought to be, to raise very acutely the question, 'Who or What is this?'" Lewis maintained that the Gospels show "there is a good deal in the character which, unless He really is what He says he is, is not loveable or even tolerable." On the other

11. I: March 26, 1940.

hand, "if He is, then of course it is another matter; nor will it be surprising if much remains puzzling to the end." He concluded by saying that "if there is anything in Christianity, we are now approaching something which will never be fully comprehensible." Therefore, he prescribed G. K. Chesterton's *Everlasting Man* and François Mauriac's *Vie de Jesus*. As an afterthought, as if the Spirit nudged Lewis, he said if painful associations from childhood interfere with Bible reading, "try it in some other language, or Moffatt's translation."[12]

Mrs. Jones had a good mind, despite her failure at Oxford. She enjoyed the give-and-take with her former tutor, and she evidently devoured the books he recommended. But her depression continued, sometimes getting much worse. On one or two occasions in 1941 and 1942, she met Lewis at his home, The Kilns. Always avoiding any appearance of wrongdoing, Lewis made certain that his housekeeper, his surrogate mother (Mrs. Moore), and several children (they took in children from London to keep them away from the German bombings) were all conspicuously present. In these counseling sessions and in a number of very long letters, Lewis tried to help Mrs. Jones see that her hope was not in fixing her problems as she saw them now. Her hope was only in Jesus Christ.

By early 1942 Grace Jones had become a Christian, but the pathway to salvation had not been easy for her, her family, or her spiritual guide. She was convinced for a long time that the "male headship" issue was a source of her marital tensions, so Lewis, with his conservative views on marriage and family, battled her head-to-head logically and biblically, showing her why marriages should not be nor ever were intended to be egalitarian.

12. Ibid.

She eventually was persuaded, and as a result decided against divorce and the breakup of her family.[13]

Mrs. Jones gradually became more stable, finding growing peace with God and her family. Because she and her husband moved into the Oxford area, Lewis had to put some rigid boundaries on the personal visits. He continued to counsel via the postal service, but increasingly his letters concluded with more than his usual "greetings to your good husband"— adding such curt phrases as "Saturday is no good for me" or "I have no leisure in my day from 8:30 a.m. to 9:30 p.m."[14]

Because the Joneses lived near Oxford, Lewis urged Grace to find a spiritual director—perhaps Lewis's own Father Walter Adams. She said she did not like the idea of confessing her sins to someone else. But Lewis replied that she confessed sins to him quite often. Why not go to someone who is set apart by God to hear you and help? Indeed, when she asked why couldn't she simply go to a friend or neighbor, he assured her she could. But the advantage with the priest is that he holds an office God appointed him to, and, unlike lay people who can be given to gossip, he will keep everything you tell him in sacred silence.[15]

Once again Lewis's logic and theology evidently prevailed. She regularly sat under the spiritual direction of a Cowley Father and stayed in touch with Lewis through the mail. From what she told Mary and me and what is revealed in the correspondence throughout most of the 1950s, Grace found increasing spiritual healing and was even able to get her eyes off of her own problems long

---

13. I: April 18, 1940; January 29, 1941; February 20, 1941; June 6, 1941; January 20, 1942.

14. I: January 20, 1942; November 5, 1953.

15. I: April 26, 1941; April 30, 1941.

enough to pray for Lewis's wife and then share Professor Lewis's grief when Joy died.[16]

In the final analysis, the Lewis-Jones relationship is a model of how Lewis served someone as a spiritual guide. He encouraged her, admitted that he too had struggles, and led her directly and logically to Jesus Christ without frontally attacking the dead-end paths she was taking. He seems to have responded to all of her letters, and he carefully answered each of her questions—usually covering her queries or arguments point by point by numbering each of his observations. Most of his advice went out in the form of suggestions, knowing full well no one will be pushed. At the same time, he handed out tough love. He labeled sin as sin. He refused to allow her to ignore clear teaching of Scripture. And while he did gratify her desire to have a few face-to-face encounters rather than just personal contact through mail, he established and maintained clear boundaries and refused to be budged, even though it was obvious she challenged those boundaries of his time and privacy. He kept pointing her to Jesus Christ and to the church, stressing that Jesus was her only hope and that she needed to be part of His body—His bride, the church. Indeed, the seeds of Lewis's powerful pamphlet "Membership" are clearly in one of his long letters to Mrs. Jones.

Lewis had the privilege of seeing some of the fruit from the massive amount of time, prayer, and thought he expended for Grace Jones. Seeing her overcome Satan's temptation to destroy first her life, then her marriage, and then the well-being of her children, he certainly celebrated each of her agonizing victories. He demonstrated his gratitude to God and showed his *agape* love for the Joneses by attending a baptism, standing as a godfather, and showering occasional gifts for spe-

16. I: May 30, 1960; September 23, 1960.

cial times such as first Communion and confirmation. Lewis knew that it is indeed "more blessed to give than to receive."[17]

C. S. Lewis's experience as a spiritual guide began with Grace Jones, but it did not end with her. By the 1940s and continuing to the day before he died, he counseled numerous souls over extended periods of time. How many he mentored we do not know. The correspondence that survives gives us a mere glimpse of how Lewis passed on to others what he had been gleaning from his devotion to prayer, Scripture, and the church, as well as the spiritual direction he received from Father Walter Adams.

Another mentoring relationship began in 1947 and lasted through 1959. Sarah Tate (not her real name) went to Oxford to study, with the goal of becoming a teacher. Because Lewis had become both famous and infamous as an Oxford tutor whose occupation was teaching literary history and criticism and whose avocation was defending and explaining Christianity, Miss Tate sent him a letter explaining why she could not believe in Christ.[18] Sensing that the Hound of Heaven already had her cornered, and observing the mettle in her spirit, Lewis immediately mounted an offense. Your trouble is that you are trying too hard, he told her, and "if you don't think it is true why do you want to believe it?" He urged her to trust God, get on with praying to him, and be as obedient to him as possible. He assured her she should keep asking questions, but

17. I: April 26, 1941.
18. These letters will be cited as Collection III, and only the dates will be given.

to let God lead her and remember "all depends on the steady attempt to obey all the time. 'He who does the will of Father shall know the doctrine.'" He confessed, "It is only fair to tell you that my impression is that you are in fact v.[ery] much nearer to belief in Christ than you suppose." He informed her that conversions come "in all sorts of ways: some sharp and catastrophic (like St. Paul, St. Augustine, or Bunyan) some very gradual and intellectual (like my own). No good predicting how God will deal with one: He has His own way with each of us. So don't worry. Continue all your efforts. . . . Keep your eye on the Helmsman."[19]

Within a few days she sought Lewis's advice on how to pray. He responded with a thoughtful and detailed answer that only a good teacher could offer.[20] A few months later he helped her as she wrestled with the incarnation. Read "St. John's Gospel and the non-Pauline epistles and keep in mind that 'it is not really you who are holding fast to Him but He to you.'" Finally, he stressed, "You are an adult student reading some v.[ery] interesting ancient records, with God to guide you. Let them and Him work. And don't get fussed and don't demand quick returns. All is obviously going pretty well."[21]

It was indeed going "pretty well." Several more letters passed over the next few months: Remember "our Lord's words, 'No man cometh to me unless the Father have drawn Him.'—well it is pretty clear that you are being drawn. . . ." In another letter he suggested she read Chesterton's *Everlasting Man*. Furthermore, because she was discussing the Bible with a rabbi and wanted to know which translation to use, he said, "Knox is better literature than Moffatt but he has to translate the Vulgate

19. III: December 31, 1947.
20. III: January 3, 1948, BL.
21. III: June 22, 1948.

143

not the GK [Greek]. This really makes little difference but the Rabbi will make play with it. . . ." Finally in June 1949 an elated Lewis could write: "Welcome Home! And thank you for writing to tell me: This has been a wonderful week, for I have just heard that my oldest friend is to be baptized on Saturday."[22]

Miss Tate continued to seek Lewis's guidance as her soul hungered for something more. She plied him with questions about the efficacy of prayer. He quoted Scripture and Pascal. Later he fed her on seeds that would one day come to fruition in some of his short pieces and ultimately *Letters to Malcolm: Chiefly on Prayer*. She begged for names of more books to read, wanting to supplement prayer and Scripture with reading that would enlarge her spirit. Lewis argued that he was "very ill qualified to give [her] a list," but nevertheless offered K. E. Kirk's *Vision of God*, E. L. McCall's *The God-Man*, and Charles Williams's *The Descent of the Dove*, plus other "old books I expect I've mentioned before: e.g. *The Imitation*, Milton's *Scale of Perfection*, . . . *Theologica Germanica*, Traherne, *Centuries of Meditations*, Lady Julian, *Revelations of Divine Love*." In other correspondence he nudged her to the church, congratulated her on adult confirmation, and explained the importance of obeying Christ by taking Holy Communion.[23]

In their ongoing correspondence, Lewis urged Sarah Tate to keep up the discipline of prayer, and he promised to pray for her. He cautioned her not to be surprised when "after a period of exaltation and comfort (such as, I think, you were having at Easter) round the next corner something horrid lies in wait for us, either in ourselves or outside. I suppose the preceding comfort was sent,

22. III: February 10, 1949; May 20, 1949; June 24, 1949.
23. III: October 21, 1949; November 3, 1949; November 9, 1949.

partly, to prepare us for the other." Always careful not to frighten or discourage, Lewis still told the truth. He wanted Sarah to know the truth that "in the world you will have tribulation. But be hopeful" for Christ has overcome the world.[24] Over the ensuing months and years Sarah obviously grew up spiritually rather quickly. Consequently her need of constant spiritual guidance from Lewis began to dwindle, just like he predicted: I have been merely "used by the Holy Spirit as a conductor," gradually growing less important while "the real thing" will never fade away.[25] As she matured spiritually she began to pass on to others what she had received. Teaching first in England, then moving back to her home in a Pacific Commonwealth country, she sought advice on how to witness to lost souls in a secular school setting. Lewis offered counsel on this and promised to pray for both her witness and strength to withstand the pressures of some intrafamily discord.[26]

Lewis's pleasure in learning of this young woman's growth became apparent in his letters to her during the 1950s. He seemed to be genuinely delighted to receive her letters containing updates on how she was making breakthroughs in witnessing to her classes of deaf children in a decidedly anti-Christian private school. She witnessed to the children and even managed to produce a small book teaching the children to pray.[27] Particularly encouraging and instructional to her must have been a letter in which Lewis urged her not to be discouraged about being in a secular environment as a witness for Christ. You might do more good "because you are not allowed to give religious

24. III: April 12, 1950.
25. III: April 4, 1950.
26. See letters in Collection III spanning summer 1950 to October 27, 1959.
27. III: December 15, 1952; February 9, 1953; May 20, 1953; December 26, 1953.

instruction in class." He said that as a child he would have been intrigued to learn his teacher believed "in a whole mass of things he wasn't allowed to teach! Let them give us the charm of mystery if they please."[28]

Her successes uplifted his soul. It was refreshing to have a "spiritual daughter" who seldom wallowed in self-pity and self-absorption, but rather searched for ways to spread the gospel to the next generation. And while Miss Tate occasionally confessed sins to Lewis, it must have encouraged her when he acknowledged battling the same problems but found peace in the grace that abounded more than the sin.[29]

The frequency of the correspondence naturally dwindled over the years. Sarah's urgency for help passed. The Holy Spirit became her guide. The two disciples walked more equally—each sharing news of the great things God was doing, sharing joy, and encouraging one another. The mentor also became a friend, and the "spiritual student" became a teacher as well as a friend who continued to learn.

The experiences of Sarah Tate on the one end of the spectrum and Grace Jones on the other symbolize bookends, with most of the other long-term correspondents stacked somewhere in between. Among these was an "American Lady" who received over one hundred letters from C. S. Lewis and then generously gave them to Clyde S. Kilby, who edited them as *Letters to an American Lady*.[30] This splendid collection reveals

28. III: March 24, 1954.
29. Ibid.
30. Kilby, *Letters*, is the source for the material in the next few paragraphs. Only direct quotations will be cited separately.

Lewis's long-lasting compassion and faithfulness to try to help one who continually wrote to him and showed rather meager progress toward maturity in Christ. Not as spiritually broken and depressed as Grace Jones, the "American Lady" nonetheless seldom grew past her massive self-concern. Although she began the correspondence in October 1950 with thanks for the books Lewis had written, the bulk of the letters are replete with complaints about physical health, including an exhaustive list of ailments. This distressed soul complained of problems with jealous coworkers, a variety of anxieties, overwork, and money problems. She begged for autographed copies of his books and a signed photograph, and hinted for monetary aid to defray costs for dental surgery. Always the victim, she frequently complained that he did not write often enough despite the fact that she probably received more letters from him than anyone did except for his lifelong friend Arthur Greeves.

On the other hand, there was a generous, sensitive heart underneath all the self-centeredness and concomitant distress. She loved animals, occasionally worried that her demands for more letters might crimp Lewis financially, and went so far as to purchase British stamps from who knows what source and then mailed them to Lewis. No doubt she could be a thorn in Lewis's side, but Father Adams had taught him how to stay grateful, stay focused, and help people just like her draw closer to Jesus Christ. Always trying to be compassionate, he sent her autographed books and the photograph she requested, and he assured her of his daily prayers for her physical and spiritual health. Lewis arranged for portions of his royalties from an American publisher to be sent directly to her; he offered countless suggestions drawn from Scripture to help her cope with life; and he took pains to explain why he could not always answer her letters within a week or two.

147

God graced Lewis with the privilege of seeing some of her spiritual victories despite the fact he knew he was called to be obedient, not successful. For instance, during one period when the American Lady was ill and became terrified of the prospect of death, Lewis wrote in his sometimes tough-love manner: "Pain is terrible, but surely you need not have fear as well? Can you see death as the friend and deliverer? It means stripping off that body which is tormenting you . . . like getting out of a dungeon. What is there to be afraid of?" He went on to say, "You have long attempted (and none of us does more) a Christian life. Your sins are confessed and absolved. Has this world been so kind to you that you should leave it with regret? There are better things ahead than any we leave behind." He concluded by assuring her that Jesus says to her "Peace, child peace. Relax. Let go. Underneath are the everlasting arms. Let go, I will catch you. Do you trust me so little?"[31]

Lewis was delighted to learn that she took the prescription, focused on Christ, and overcame her fear. "Tho' horrified at your sufferings, I am overjoyed at the blessed change in your attitude about death. This is a bigger stride forward than perhaps you yourself yet know."[32] Her strides were indeed good. She obviously got out of herself and thanked him profusely for all he had done for her over the years. Rather certain she was on the brink of death, she wanted to clear her accounts and say goodbye. Lewis responded in his typically generous way: "You say too much of the very little I have been able to do for you."[33]

Ironically, she recovered and lived on for quite a few more years. He, on the other hand, wrote a letter to her

31. Kilby, *Letters*, June 17, 1963, 114.
32. Ibid., June 25, 1963, 115–16.
33. Ibid.

from the chair in which he had to remain twenty-four hours a day, while confined for a time to the Acland Nursing Home in Oxford. Quite ill, unable to lie flat on a bed, and full of infection from a urinary tract infection, he gathered what strength he had to write her one more letter. He thanked her for her letter but said his brother was away and therefore he had to handle all his correspondence by himself. "So you must expect my letters to be very few and very short. More a wave of the hand than a letter."[34] Dated August 30, 1963, this was his last letter to the "American Lady."

C. S. Lewis carried on a fascinating correspondence with an Italian Roman Catholic priest, Don Giovanni Calabria, from 1947 until 1954, when the Italian padre died.[35] This collection is remarkable in many ways; among other things it points up the marked differences between a good Catholic and a good Anglican with High Church leanings. Nevertheless, the men became bonded friends, although they never met in person. Although the correspondence dwells on ecumenical issues and searching for bridges between the traditions, what is beautiful is the way each man believes that prayer changes things on this earth. These two devout believers exchange prayer requests and celebrate God's goodness in answer to their petitions. Yet even in this unusual series of letters Lewis emerges as a sensitive spiritual guide to the Italian priest. Certainly Father Don Giovanni invites the English layman's prayers and

34. Kilby, *Letters*, August 30, 1963, 121.

35. The correspondence was in Latin, and the original Latin letters with translations in English by Martin Moynihan were published by Servant Books in Ann Arbor, Michigan, and reprinted in 1998 by St. Augustine's Press.

counsel. And if Lewis is somewhat disinclined to offer spiritual advice to an ordained priest, he does so despite this reluctance. "Your intercessions on my behalf," Lewis begins, give him the boldness "to say . . . something that a layman ought scarcely to say to a priest nor a junior to a senior (on the other hand, out of the mouths of babes: indeed, as once to Balaam, out of the mouth of an ass!)." Lewis the spiritual counselor at once admonished and exhorted his long-distance friend: "You write too much about your own sins. Beware (permit me, my dearest Father, to say beware) lest humility should pass over into anxiety or sadness. It is bidden us to 'rejoice and always rejoice.' Jesus has cancelled the handwriting which was against us." Then, quoting a phrase from the liturgy of the Eucharist that that priest would have said and that Lewis heard every Sunday—"Lift up your hearts!" In conclusion Lewis wrote,

> "Permit me, I pray you, these stammerings. You are ever in my prayers."[36]

In the 1950s and early 1960s Professor Lewis carried on a fascinating correspondence with an American woman whose husband had just died. A strong encourager but always a wise and honest counselor, he assured her of his prayers and acknowledged, "I can well believe that you were divinely supported at the time of your terrible calamity. People often are. It is afterwards, where the new and bleaker life is beginning to be a routine, that one often feels one has been left rather unaided. I am sure one is not really so. God's presence is not the

36. CSL to Don Giovanni, December 26, 1951, in Moynihan, *Letters*, 69–70.

same as the feeling of God's presence and He may be doing most for us when we think He is doing least." He goes on to prepare her for a season of loneliness that he is "pretty sure" is one of the ways by which we can grow spiritually. After some more words of wisdom, he encourages her: "Be very regular in your prayer and communion; and don't value special 'guidances' any more than what comes thro' ordinary Christian teaching, conscience, and prudence."[37]

Over the next few years Lewis offered words of spiritual hope and encouragement, recommended that she read George MacDonald, assured her she had been in his "daily prayers ever since [her] first letter," and sent her an autographed *Till We Have Faces*. He also encouraged her as she began publishing articles on Christian topics and celebrated her remarriage six years after the death of her first husband. Finally, when she tried to thank him for his spiritual counsel by offering an unspecified gift, he wrote: "Many thanks for the kind thought but don't send me a present. There are so very few things I want that presents embarrass me, because I know I can't enjoy them as the donors intend."[38]

Beginning in August 1949 and continuing until the day before he died, C. S. Lewis carried on an illuminative correspondence with another woman in the United States. For Lewis's part, he wrote nearly eighty letters. This collection of epistles shows Lewis at his best as a spiritual director—offering warm encouragement, clear warnings,

37. CSL to Mrs. A. J. McCaslin (later Ward), August 2, 1954.
38. CSL to Mrs. A. J. McCaslin (later Ward), September 19, 1954; November 15, 1956; February 25, 1957; January 12, 1962; November 24, 1961; November 16, 1962.

and direct challenges designed to uplift and strengthen the soul. These letters reveal much about Lewis and his struggles, because with this essentially healthy soul he felt completely comfortable about being transparent with his own needs. He obviously believed that this woman was a good and growing soul whose prayers for him and his wife, Joy, would be heard on high. He enjoyed a bit of intellectual jousting with her because she was neither easily offended nor unable to return his intellectual serve. And she was one of the few correspondents—if letters that survive are representative—who did much more than take. To be sure, Lewis gave her counsel and even advice when she sought it. On the other hand she stimulated his thinking and had a book or two to recommend to him.

The fourteen-year correspondence between C. S. Lewis and Mrs. Van Deusen began in 1949 when she wrote to urge him to write a book on prayer. Perhaps she planted the seed of what eventually grew into *Letters to Malcolm: Chiefly on Prayer* that appeared a decade and a half later. If her letter served as an impetus for such an endeavor, Lewis gave no indication in his response: "I think it would be rather 'cheek' on my part . . . I don't feel I could write a book on prayer."[39]

More correspondence followed on prayer, and then in summer 1950 she brought forth some questions she had on Holy Communion, the local church, and healing prayer. Lewis got right to the point on Communion: Our Lord requires it. Regarding the church, service to the Lord is no substitute for gathering in a worshipful community. Paraphrasing his essay on the church written five years before, Lewis emphatically informed her that for Christians there

39. CSL to Mrs. Van Deusen (her real name), September 9, 1949.

is no such thing as solitary religion. Of course you should practice private prayer and reading, but you don't forsake meeting together. Furthermore, one has no right to look for a community of affinity. 1 Corinthians 12 says we are brought together as organs, not members. Being together with those we do not enjoy causes us to be humble.[40]

Healing became for Van Deusen a topic larger than the way Lewis at first discussed it. Scripture promised it to the church, he noted, but he would be somewhat suspicious of "great movements in one place." Nevertheless, he acknowledged he "could be wrong."[41] Mrs. Van Deusen persisted. She questioned if healing ministry is done out of spiritual pride or sincerity. Lewis returned to Scripture, as he usually did. We are "instructed" to lay on hands and pray for healing. And if healing occurs, there is no way to prove that prayer caused it or that the healing would have come anyway. The efficacy of prayer cannot be measured. The truth, according to Lewis, is this: "All our prayers are united with Christ's perpetual prayer and are part of the Church's prayer." Furthermore, "in prayer for people one dislikes I find it v.[ery] helpful to remember that one is joining in His prayer for them."[42]

Lewis provided his view on how Christians should deal with sinners, sin, and consequences of sin. It is never sinful to attempt to remove some natural consequences of sin. For instance, if a young woman fornicates and becomes pregnant, we should provide a bed in a maternity ward, help place a roof over her head, and provide an education if she needs it. This is simple Christian charity. But it is "wrong to remove them [consequences] by abortion or infanticide."[43]

40. CSL to Mrs. Van Deusen, July 1, 1950.
41. Ibid.
42. CSL to Mrs. Van Deusen, January 5, 1951.
43. CSL to Mrs. Van Deusen, July 2, 1951.

Within two years of corresponding with this American, he was comfortable and trustful enough to be unusually transparent about his personal life. He wrote that Chad Walsh, who had written the biography *C. S. Lewis: Apostle to the Skeptics* a year and half earlier, did not know much about his private life. "Strictly between ourselves, I have lived most of it (that is now over) in a house wh.[ich] was hardly ever at peace for 24 hours, amid senseless wrangling, lyings, backbiting, follies, and tears. I never went home without a feeling of terror as to what appalling situation might have developed in my absence."[44] Lewis was referring to life at his house when Mrs. Moore was alive. She disrupted relationships among all the hired help and made the environment extremely difficult for him and Warren.

Such candor on Lewis's part enabled him to identify with his friend. Consequently, he could be heard more readily when he offered advice to be patient with family problems. "I suppose one thing we must do about these minor crises is to get them into perspective. At the moment when the nuisance . . . is at its worst, remember that (at that precise moment) people are dying in pain and others are at their bedside, and in China children are starving and men in prison camps and some of them being tortured."[45] In the same vein he could tell her that another family member's marital problems needed to be seen in a biblical light. "It sounds to me as if [your family member] had a pretty good [spouse] on the whole. So much matrimonial misery comes to me in mail that I feel those whose partner has no worse fault than being stupider than themselves may be said to have drawn a prize! It hardly amounts to a problem. I take it that in every marriage natural love sooner or later, in high or

44. CSL to Mrs. Van Deusen, April 18, 1951.
45. CSL to Mrs. Van Deusen, September 13, 1962.

low degree, comes up against difficulties (if only the difficulty that the original state of 'being in Love' dies a natural death) which face it will either turn into dislike or else turn into Christian charity. For all our natural feelings are, not resting places, but *points d'affui*, springboards. One always has to go on from them or fall back from them." He then urged her to have the complainer read 1 Peter 4:12.[46]

Lewis's Van Deusen letters are replete with recommendations and discussions of books. He admitted that the books he had written were only his perspective on the faith; therefore, the popular works of "à Kempis, Bunyan, Chesterton, Alice Meynell, Otto, William Law, Coventry Patmore, Dante, might be good supplements." In another letter he urged Mrs. Van Deusen to read George Herbert's *The Temple*, and later he acknowledged that what we know, "when said by someone else, becomes suddenly operative," and that is why the prose of Francis de Sales and poetry of George Herbert were so important to him.[47] Van Deusen had her recommendation for Lewis as well. He agreed Evelyn Underhill was a good author, but he had not read *Worship*. In fact, he confessed, "You have no idea how many books written in this century are unknown to me."[48]

This exchange of letters includes many of Lewis's usual prescriptions for soul care: practice the presence of God, embrace mystery when Scripture appears contradictory, do not demand or expect feelings, but be grateful when they come, and be radically obedient in all things. But this series of correspondence also reveals Lewis's wide-ranging versatility and wisdom. When she inquired about

46. CSL to Mrs. Van Deusen, July 23, 1953.
47. CSL to Mrs. Van Deusen, June 11, 1951; July 7, 1951; December 26, 1951.
48. CSL to Mrs. Van Deusen, September 6, 1959.

psychiatry Lewis described it as surgery—and surgery inflicts wounds. "But all psychiatrists are not agreed as to the proper shape of the soul: when their ideas of that proper shape are based on heathen or materialistic philosophy, they may be aiming at a shape we sh[ou]ld. strongly disapprove. One wants a Christian psychiatrist." But beware, he cautioned, there are not many.[49]

Lewis also had some excellent insights on aged people. Mrs. Van Deusen, who seemed to be very happily married, unlike many correspondents, undertook an enterprise with her husband that involved the founding of a "rest-home where people in psychological difficulties could get" help. Everything "depends on the quality of the individual helpers," and he suspected you can find them only through prayer. Also, whether or not they should embark on this "Project" must be discerned in prayer. "I suppose the deeper one's own life of prayer and sacrament the more trustworthy one's judgment will be." Her husband's aunt seemed to be a case that prodded the couple to establish a facility because none seemed to exist that combined full care and treatment for dementia. Lewis admitted he had "been in v.[ery] close contact with a case like that: it is harrowing. My doctor (a v.[ery] serious Christian) kept reminding me that so much of an old person's speech and behavior must really be treated as a medical and not a spiritual fact: that, as an organism decays, the true state of the soul can less express itself thro' it. So that things may be neither so miserable (nor so wicked, we must sometimes add) as they seem."[50]

Mrs. Van Deusen and her husband were interested in more than the "Project" to help aged people suffering from dementia; they looked for effective ways to

49. CSL to Mrs. Van Deusen, June 10, 1952.
50. CSL to Mrs. Van Deusen, October 10, 1953.

do evangelism. When Lewis was asked how he saw the call to witness, he said we "sin" if we refuse because we are fearful of looking foolish. But remaining silent because we don't want to provide further evidence that Christians are bothersome people to be avoided, that is a different matter. "I am quite sure that an important bit of evangelism from a comparative stranger w[oul]d. not have done me any good when I was an unbeliever."[51] In short, discernment and good judgment are necessary in each situation.

Discernment and common sense applied to more than personal evangelism. To Lewis's mind, the same thing applied to the rule of life. "If one is asked for advice, then, and then only, one has to have an opinion about the exact rule of life which w[oul]d. suit some other Christians. Otherwise, I think the rule is to mind one's own business. St. Paul goes farther than this: it may even be proper at times to adopt practices which you yourself think unnecessary, and which are unnecessary to you, if your difference on such points is a stumbling block to the Christians you find yourself among." He prescribed Romans 14.[52]

Lewis used the trans-Atlantic mail service to offer advice on many other issues that Mrs. Van Deusen brought up, but because the relationship was not totally one-sided he truly enjoyed the give-and-take with Van Deusen. This can be seen in one letter where he wrote: "I was extremely glad to get your letter. I was beginning to feel that my own had been presumptuous and intolerable and had been praying not that it might do good but that it might not do harm. Whether I was right or wrong, you come out of it with flying colours: if few can give good advice, fewer still can hear with patience advice either good or bad."[53] She had taken his

51. CSL to Mrs. Van Deusen, April 7, 1953.
52. CSL to Mrs. Van Deusen, June 28, 1953.

directness in good stride, and this is why he confided a number of personal things. He respected her maturity, good sense, and ever deepening spirituality. He sought her and her husband's prayers for his physical ailments, including sinusitis, neuritis, and kidney infections. He sought their prayer for Joy, and he asked prayer for strength to handle the mail (without ever hinting that her letters were unwelcome). He shared that he loathed being "alone in the house"—no doubt because he disliked doing the chores alone, especially when he was ill.[54] But being alone actually made this man who required privacy to read, write, think, and pray quite lonely. Despite his need to be alone, Lewis had people underfoot at The Kilns almost continuously from the time he and his brother, Warren, bought the place in 1931. There were Warren, Maude and Len Miller (the housekeeper and her husband), Fred Paxford (the gardener and handyman), Janie King Moore (Jack's best friend's mother, whom he cared for like a mother after her son's death in World War I), Mrs. Moore's daughter Maureen, an assortment of London children escaping the Nazi blitz during World War II, and finally his wife, Joy, and her two sons, David and Douglas.

Lewis's last letter to Mrs.Van Deusen, his pen friend for nearly a decade and a half, was written November 21, 1963, one day before he died. In retrospect, it is markedly appropriate. She had evidently written to confide the deep sense of dislocation she and her husband felt as they were moving to a new housing situation more appropriate for their current chapter in life.

I think I share, to excess, your feeling about a move. By nature I demand from the arrangements of this world

53. CSL to Mrs. Van Deusen, October 10, 1953.
54. CSL to Mrs. Van Deusen, June 20, 1963.

just that permanence which God has expressly refused to give them. It is not merely the nuisance and expense of any big change in one's way of life that I dread. It is also the psychological uprooting and the feeling—to me, and to you, intensely unwelcome—of having ended a chapter. One more portion of oneself slipping away into the past! I would like everything to be immemorial—to have the same old horizons, the same garden, the same smells and sounds, always there, changeless. The old wine is to be always better. That is, I desire the "abiding city" where I well know it is not and ought not to be found. I suppose all these changes sh[oul]d. prepare us for the far greater change which has drawn nearer ever since I began this letter. We must "sit light" not only to Life itself but to all its phases. The useless word is "Encore!"

This was probably Professor Lewis's last letter.

C. S. Lewis's radical obedience bore much fruit. Thousands of letters were written to innumerable souls. The wisdom, prescriptions for healing, and care of souls, as well as examples of compassion and patience, are as fresh and applicable today as when he wrote them a generation ago.

8

LEGACY

"The Real Thing Will Live on after the Shine of My Books Dies"

Few twentieth-century Christians in the English-speaking world have had a wider range of influence on souls than C. S. Lewis. And like saints of earlier eras, he deliberately and faithfully focused on the depth of his relationship with Christ Jesus. Consequently, the Holy Spirit has taken care of the breadth of his influence. That Mr. Lewis paid scant attention to his widespread fame, or grasped any real sense that his profound contribution to the rescue and care of souls would be long-lasting, is evidenced by a comment Lewis made to Owen Barfield.

This long-time friend and legal advisor raised the topic of Lewis's growing fame and the widespread popularity of his books. That Lewis did not take himself too seriously is evidenced by these terse words: "the Real Thing will live on after the shine of my books dies."[1]

Lewis was no fool, but he was no prophet either. He could not have been more wrong about the market for his books. His writings sell more today than they ever did during his lifetime. Furthermore, the public is so hungry for more Lewis that any piece of unpublished material finds an eager readership once it appears in print. There seems to be a deep reservoir of unpublished Lewis writings, because "new" material—sometimes combined with a few previously published pieces—finds its way into book form with amazing regularity. Indeed, Barfield told me that the continuous flow of Lewis's works after his death caused his old friend and sometimes critic J. R. R. Tolkien to quip that Lewis was the only man he ever knew who published more after his death than when he lived. And in case anyone assumed the creator of *The Hobbit* and *The Lord of the Rings* tended to exaggerate, thirteen different volumes containing at least some previously unpublished Lewis material went on sale before Tolkien died in 1973.

If C. S. Lewis could not foresee the next generation's hunger for his books, he did understand the difference between temporal and eternal issues. He knew beyond the shadow of a doubt that his writing would one day go the way of all books. And his wisdom, after all, became the impetus for his work and its powerful effect on souls nearly a half-century after his passing.

1. Barfield related these words to me during our many discussions.

Lewis's desire—already in 1940—to learn from a man hidden away in an Anglican monastery on the edge of Oxford—a monk shrouded in a cloak of obscurity by all temporal standards, yet one whose soul radiated the preeminence of Christ—helped shape Lewis's true legacy. With Father Walter Adams's encouragement Lewis became determined to keep his focus on the Lord Jesus Christ and not let the gaze stray. Adams taught Lewis and others called to the care of souls that "we ought always to feel how much more important our prayers are" than anything we do. "We must drink in from God what ever we would give forth from Him. It must come to us straight from God. We cannot expect to move the hearts of others save by the power of the Holy Ghost."[2]

Our own "eagerness for success," even in the ministry of soul care, "thwarts the manifestation of the Resurrection power, by which alone the truly mortified life is to be perfected. The Resurrection life is hidden from the world, but we can long for that which the world can and will appreciate. . . . May we have grace to know more and more of His Resurrection power, to live with the doors shut, with hearts truly enclosed."[3]

Lewis increasingly stood in the comfort of knowing that Christ is all in all and that anything that is not of him, by him, and for him will burn up in the end times if not much sooner. He jotted these words in his personal copy of the Book of Common Prayer: "What seems to be you at the time, to be your own effort, must in fact be grace."[4] In the same vein, as Owen Barfield observed,

2. See Adams's collection of his thoughts, combined with quotations from teachings of R. M. Benson, in a 28-page booklet, *Thoughts from the Notebooks of a Priest Religious*, assembled and printed in 1949 by the Faith Press in London. See 15–16.

3. Ibid.

4. The words are inscribed in Lewis's prayer book that is part of the Lewis collection at the Wade Center.

Lewis took less interest in himself as the years passed. "Self-knowledge, for him," came to nothing more than "recognition of his own weaknesses and shortcomings."[5] The core of what Lewis learned and passed on to us in his concluding paragraph of *Mere Christianity* still speaks like words from a far country, so foreign are they to our self-absorbed lives and culture:

> . . . There must be a real giving up of the self. You must throw it away "blindly" so to speak. Christ will indeed give you a real personality: but you must not go to Him for the sake of that. As long as your own personality is what you are bothering about you are not going to Him at all. . . . Give up yourself, and you will find your real self. Lose your life and you will save it.

Lewis emphatically maintained that our personal ambitions and wishes must be mortified. Submit everything—"every fibre of your being, and you will find eternal life." Hold back nothing.

> Nothing that you have not given away will ever be really yours. Nothing in you that has not died will ever be raised from the dead. Look for yourself, and you will find in the long run only hatred, loneliness, despair, rage, ruin and decay. But look for Christ and you find Him, and with Him everything else thrown in.[6]

C. S. Lewis's earthly end came on Friday, November 22, 1963, one week before his sixty-fourth birthday. Warren Lewis remembered that the day "began much as other days: there was breakfast, then letters and the

---

5. See Barfield's "Introduction" to *Light on Lewis*, xvi.
6. CSL, *Mere Christianity*, 175.

crossword puzzle." The duties of the midday were carried out and followed by lunch. Jack, still plagued by fever from a lingering urinary tract infection, dozed off in his chair. Warren recalled, "I suggested he would be more comfortable in bed, and he went there. At four I took in his tea and found him drowsy but comfortable. Our few words then were the last: at five-thirty I heard a crash and ran in, to find him lying unconscious at the foot of his bed. He ceased to breathe some three or four minutes later."[7]

Two years later Owen Barfield confessed that despite their close and long-standing relationship, "He stood before me as a mystery as solidly as he stood beside me as a friend."[8] Perhaps C. S. Lewis's most enduring legacy will be that in the final analysis we do not see him clearly at all, because he stands in the shadows, as it were, like a soldier at a fork in the road on the edge of a combat zone. He briskly motions the troops on toward the proper direction. No one really sees or pays close attention to the one directing the troops. They are too preoccupied with the action that lies ahead.

7. WHL, "Memoir," in WHL, *Letters*, 25.
8. Barfield, "Introduction," *Light on Lewis*, xxi.

SELECTED BIBLIOGRAPHY

Books Written by C. S. Lewis

Autobiography

All My Road Before Me: The Diary of C. S. Lewis, 1922–1927
  (1992), ed. by Walter Hooper
A Grief Observed (1961)
Surprised by Joy: The Shape of My Early Life (1955)

Children's Fiction

Boxen: The Imaginary World of the Young C. S. Lewis (1986),
  ed. by Walter Hooper
The Horse and His Boy (1956)
The Last Battle: A Story for Children (1956)
The Lion the Witch and the Wardrobe: A Story for Children
  (1950)
The Magician's Nephew (1955)
Prince Caspian: The Return to Narnia (1951)
The Silver Chair (1953)
The Voyage of the "Dawn Treader" (1952)

Adult Fiction

The Great Divorce: A Drama (1945)

Out of the Silent Planet (1938)

Perelandra: A Novel (1943)

The Pilgrim's Regress: An Allegorical Apology for Christianity, Reason and Romanticism (1933)

The Screwtape Letters (1942, *Screwtape Proposes a Toast* added in 1961)

That Hideous Strength: A Modern Fairy-Tale for Grown-Ups (1945)

Till We Have Faces: A Myth Retold (1956)

Nonfiction

The Abolition of Man (1943)

The Allegory of Love: A Study of Medieval Tradition (1936)

Beyond Personality: The Christian Idea of God (1944)

The Case for Christianity, or Broadcast Talks (1942)

Christian Behavior: A Further Series of Broadcast Talks (1943)

The Discarded Image: An Introduction to Medieval and Renaissance Literature (1964)

English Literature in the Sixteenth Century, Excluding Drama (1954)

An Experiment in Criticism (1961)

The Four Loves (1960)

Letters to Malcolm: Chiefly on Prayer (1964)

Mere Christianity (1952)

Miracles: A Preliminary Study (1947) [chapter three revised in 1960]

The Personal Heresy: A Controvesy (1939), with E. M. W. Tillyard

A Preface to "Paradise Lost" (1942)

The Problem of Pain (1940)

Reflections on the Psalms (1958)

Spenser's Images of Life (1967), ed. by Alastair Fowler
Studies in Words (1960)

Books of Essays Written by C. S. Lewis

Christian Reflections (1967), ed. by Walter Hooper
Fern-Seed and Elephants and Other Essays on Christianity (1975), ed. by Walter Hooper
God in the Dock: Essays on Theology and Ethics (1970) [*Undeceptions in England*] ed. by Walter Hooper
Of Other Worlds: Essays and Stories (1966), ed. by Walter Hooper
Present Concerns (1986), ed. by Walter Hooper
Rehabilitations and Other Essays (1939)
Selected Literary Essays (1969), ed. by Walter Hooper
Studies in Medieval and Renaissance Literature (1966), ed. by Walter Hooper
They Asked for a Paper: Papers and Addresses (1962)
The Weight of Glory and Other Addresses (1980), expanded and ed. by Walter Hooper
The World's Last Night and Other Essays (1960)

Books of Poetry and Verse

Dymer (1926) [originally published under the pseudonym Clive Hamilton]
Narrative Poems (1969), ed. by Walter Hooper
Poems (1964), ed. by Walter Hooper
Spirits in Bondage: A Cycle of Lyrics (1919) [originally published under the pseudonym Clive Hamilton]

Books Edited by C. S. Lewis

Arthurian Torso (1948)
Essays Presented to Charles Williams (1947)
George MacDonald: An Anthology (1946)

Books of Letters

Collected Letters of C. S. Lewis Vol. 1: Family Letters, 1905–1931 (2000), ed. by Walter Hooper

Collected Letters of C. S. Lewis Vol. 2: Books, Broadcasts and War 1931–1949 (2004), ed. by Walter Hooper

Letters to an American Lady (1967), ed. by Clyde S. Kilby

Letters to Children (1985), ed. by Lyle W. Dorsett and Marjorie Lamp Mead

Letters of C. S. Lewis (1966), ed. by Warren H. Lewis

They Stand Together: The Letters of C. S. Lewis to Arthur Greeves, 1914–1963 (1979), ed. by Walter Hooper

The Latin Letters of C. S. Lewis (1987), ed. by Martin Moynihan

Anthologies

Dorsett, Lyle W., ed. *The Essential C. S. Lewis* (1996)

Goffar, Janine. *The C. S. Lewis Index: A Comprehensive Guide to Lewis's Writings and Ideas* (1998)

Kilby, Clyde S., ed. *A Mind Awake: An Anthology of C. S. Lewis* (1968)

Martindale, Wayne and Jerry Root, eds. *The Quotable Lewis* (1990)

Schultz, Jeffrey D. and John G. West, eds. *The C. S. Lewis Readers' Encyclopedia* (1998)

Major Secondary Works

Adey, Lionel. *C. S. Lewis's "Great War" with Owen Barfield* (1978)

___. *C. S. Lewis: Writer, Dreamer and Mentor* (1998)

Aeschliman, Michael D. *The Restitution of Man: C. S. Lewis and the Case Against Scientism* (1983)

Arnott, Anne. *The Secret Country of C. S. Lewis* (1975)

Barratt, David. *C. S. Lewis and His World* (1987)

Beversluis, John. *C. S. Lewis and the Search for Rational Religion* (1985)

Bleakley, David. *C. S. Lewis: At Home in Ireland* (1998)

Bramlett, Perry. *C. S. Lewis: Life at the Center* (1996)

Bresland, Ronald W. *The Backward Glance: C. S. Lewis and Ireland* (1999)

Burson, Scott R. and Jerry C. Walls. *C. S. Lewis and Francis Schaeffer: Lessons for a New Century from the Most Influential Apologists of our Time* (1998)

Carnell, Corbin Scott. *Bright Shadow of Reality: Spiritual Longing in C. S. Lewis* (1999)

Carpenter, Humphrey. *The Inklings* (1979)

Christensen, Michael J. *C. S. Lewis on Scripture* (1979)

Christopher, Joe R. *C. S. Lewis* (1987)

Como, James. *Branches to Heaven: The Geniuses of C. S. Lewis* (1998)

___, ed. *C. S. Lewis at the Breakfast Table* (1979)

Cording, Ruth James. *C. S. Lewis: A Celebration of His Early Life* (2000)

Corren, Michael. *The Man Who Created Narnia: The Story of C. S. Lewis* (1994)

Cunningham, Richard B. *C. S. Lewis: Defender of the Faith* (1967)

Derrick, Christopher. *C. S. Lewis and the Church of Rome* (1981)

Ditchfield, Christin. *A Family Guide to Narnia: Biblical Truths in C. S. Lewis's the Chronicles of Narnia* (2003)

Dorsett, Lyle W. *And God Came In: The Extraordinary Story of Joy Davidman, Her Life and Marriage to C. S. Lewis* (1983)

Downing, David C. *The Most Reluctant Convert: C. S. Lewis' Journey to Faith* (2002)

Duncan, John Ryan. *The Magic Never Ends: An Oral History of the Life and Work of C. S. Lewis* (2001)

Edwards, Bruce L., Jr. *A Rhetoric of Reading: C. S. Lewis's Defense of Western Literacy* (1986)

Ford, Paul F. *Companion to Narnia* (1980)

Gibb, Jocelyn, ed. *Light on C. S. Lewis* (1965)

Gibson, Evan K. *Spinner of Tales: A Guide to His Fiction* (1980)

Glaspey, Terry W. *Not a Tame Lion: The Spiritual Legacy of C. S. Lewis* (1996)

Glover, Donald E. *C. S. Lewis: The Art of Enchantment* (1981)

Gormley, Beatrice. *C. S. Lewis: Christian and Storyteller* (1997)

Graham, David. *We Remember C. S. Lewis: Essays and Memories* (2001)

Green, Roger Lancelyn, and Walter Hooper. *C. S. Lewis: A Biography* (1974)

Gresham, Douglas H. *Lenten Lands: My Childhood with Joy Davidman & C. S. Lewis* (1990)

Griffin, William. *Clive Staples Lewis: A Dramatic Life* (1986)

___. *C. S. Lewis: Spirituality for Mere Christians* (1998)

Hannay, Margaret Patterson. *C. S. Lewis* (1981)

Harries, Richard. *C. S. Lewis: The Man and His God* (1987)

Hart, Dabney Adams. *Through the Open Door: A New Look at C. S. Lewis* (1984)

Holmer, Paul L. *C. S. Lewis: The Shape of His Faith and Thought* (1976)

Hooper Walter, ed. *C. S. Lewis Companion and Guide: A Delightful Compedium of Information of the Life and Writing of the Twentieth-Century's Favorite Christian Writer* (1998)

___. *Past Watchful Dragons: The Narnian Chronicles of C. S. Lewis* (1979)

Howard, Thomas. *The Achievement of C. S. Lewis* (1980)

Keefe, Caroline. *C. S. Lewis: Speaker and Teacher* (1971)

Kilby, Clyde S. *The Christian World of C. S. Lewis* (1964)

___. *Images of Salvation in the Fiction of C. S. Lewis* (1978)

___, and Marjorie Lamp Mead, eds. *Brothers and Friends: The Diaries of Major William Hamilton Lewis* (1982)

___. *C. S. Lewis: Images of His World* (1973)

King, Don W. *C. S. Lewis, Poet: The Legacy of His Poetic Impulse* (2001)

Kort, Wesley. *C. S. Lewis: Then and Now* (2001)

Kreeft, Peter. *C. S. Lewis: A Critical Essay* (1969)

___. *C. S. Lewis for the Third Millennium* (1994)

___. *The Shadow Lands of C. S. Lewis: The Man Behind the Movie* (1994)

Lawlor, John. *C. S. Lewis: Memories and Reflections* (1998)

Lindskoog, Kathryn A. *C. S. Lewis: Mere Christian* (1987)

___. *The Lion of Judah in Never-Never Land: God, Man and Nature in C. S. Lewis's Narnia Tales* (1973)

Markos, Louis. *Lewis Agonistes: How C. S. Lewis Can Train Us to Wrestle with the Modern and Postmodern World* (2003)

Martin, Thomas L. *Reading the Classics with C. S. Lewis* (2000)

Mastrolia, Arthur. *C. S. Lewis and the Blessed Virgin Mary: Uncovering a "Marian Attitude"* (2000)

Menuge, Angus J. L. *C. S. Lewis: Lightbearer in the Shadowlands: The Evangelistic Vision of C. S. Lewis* (1997)

Mills, David, ed. *Pilgrims' Guide: C. S. Lewis and the Art of Witness* (1998)

Milward, Peter. *A Challenge to C. S. Lewis* (1995)

Morris, A. Clifford. *Miles and Miles: Some Reminiscences of an Oxford Taxi Driver and Private Car Home Service Chauffeur* (1964)

Meilaender, Gilbert. *The Taste for the Other: The Social and Ethical Thought of C. S. Lewis* (1978)

Myers, Doris T. *C. S. Lewis in Context* (1994)

Nicholi, Armand J., Jr. *The Question of God: C. S. Lewis and Sigmund Freud Debate God, Love, Sex, and the Meaning of Life* (2003)

Payne, Leanne. *Real Presence: The Holy Spirit in the Works of C. S. Lewis* (1979)

Pearce, Joseph. *C. S. Lewis and the Catholic Church* (2003)

Peters, John. *C. S. Lewis: The Man and His Achievement* (1985)

Phillips, Justin. *C. S. Lewis at the BBC: Messages of Hope in the Darkness of War* (2003)

Purtill, Richard. *C. S. Lewis's Case for the Christian Faith* (1981)

Reed, Gerald. *C. S. Lewis and the Bright Shadow of Holiness* (1999)

___. *C. S. Lewis Explores Vice and Virtue* (2001)

Reppert, Victor. *C. S. Lewis' Dangerous Idea: A Philosophical Defense of Lewis's Argument from Reason* (2003)

Rort, Wesley, A. *C. S. Lewis: Then and Now* (2001)

Sammons, Martha C. *A Guide Through C. S. Lewis's Space Trilogy* (1980)

___. *A Guide Through Narnia* (1979)

Sayer, George. *Jack: A Life of C. S. Lewis* (1988, revised 1994)

Schakel, Peter J. *Reading with a Heart: The Way into Narnia* (1979)

___. *Reason and Imagination in C. S. Lewis: A Study of Till We Have Faces* (1984)

___, and Charles A. Huttar, eds. *Word and Story in C. S. Lewis* (1991)

Schofield, Stephen, ed. *In Search of C. S. Lewis* (1983)

Sibley, Brian. *C. S. Lewis through the Shadowlands: The Story of His Life with Joy Davidman* (1994)

Skinner, Andrew C., and Robert L. Millet, eds. *C. S. Lewis: The Man and His Message* (1999)

Smith, Robert H. *Patches of Godlight: The Pattern of Thought in C. S. Lewis* (1981)

Takeno, Kazuo. *A Study of C. S. Lewis's Doctrine of God* (1984)

Taliaferro, Charles C. *Praying with C. S. Lewis* (1998)

Vanauken, Sheldon. *A Severe Mercy* (1978)

Vaus, Will. *Mere Theology: A Guide to the Thought of C. S. Lewis* (2004)

Walmsley, Lesley, ed. *C. S. Lewis: Essay Collection and Other Short Pieces* (2000)

Walsh, Chad. *C. S. Lewis: Apostle to the Skeptics* (1949)

White, Michael. *C. S. Lewis: A Life* (2004)

White, William Luther. *The Image of Man in C. S. Lewis* (1969)

Willis, John Randolph. *Pleasures Forevermore: The Theology of C. S. Lewis* (1983)

Other Works Related to C. S. Lewis's Spiritual Formation

Works by Walter Adams

Thoughts from the Note-Books of a Priest Religious (1953)

Triumphant in Suffering: A Study in Reparation (1951)

Works on or by Richard Meux Benson

Benson, R. M. *Bible Teachings: The Discourse at Capernaum: S. John VI* (1898)

___. *In the Name of Jesus. A Sermon Preached Before the University of Oxford on the Fifth Sunday after Epiphany, 1865* (1865)

___. *Instructions on the Religious Life* (1935)

___. *Religious Vocation* (1939)

___. *Spiritual Letters of Richard Meux Benson*, ed. by W. H. Longridge (1924)

___. *The War-Songs of the Prince of Peace: A Devotional Commentary on the Psalter*, 2 vol. (1901)

Smith, Martin, ed. *Benson of Cowley* (1980)

Woodgate, M. V. *Father Benson: Founder of the Cowley Fathers* (1953)

INDEX